ORGANIZATIONAL PARADOXES

ORGANIZATIONAL PARADOXES THEORY & PRACTICE

Medhanie Gaim, Stewart R. Clegg and Miguel Pina e Cunha

S Sage

S Sage

1 Oliver's Yard
55 City Road
London EC1Y 1SP

2455 Teller Road
Thousand Oaks
California 91320

Unit No 323-333, Third Floor, F-Block
International Trade Tower
Nehru Place, New Delhi – 110 019

8 Marina View Suite 43-053
Asia Square Tower 1
Singapore 018960

Publisher: Kirsty Smy
Assistant Editor: Charlotte Hegley
Production editor: Rabia Barkatulla
Copyeditor: Diana Chambers
Proofreader: William Baginsky
Indexer: Elizabeth Ball
Marketing manager: Lucia Sweet
Cover design: Francis Kenney
Typeset by: C&M Digitals (P) Ltd, Chennai, India

Library of Congress Control Number: 2023947371

British Library Cataloguing in Publication data

A catalogue record for this book is available from the British Library.

ISBN 978-1-5297-9190-7
ISBN 978-1-5297-9189-1 (pbk)

Contents

List of Figures

List of Tables

List of Boxes

About the Authors

Medhanie Gaim (PhD) is Associate Professor of Management at Umeå School of Business, Economics and Statistics, Sweden. His research focuses on paradox theory (its beauty and absurdity) and entrepreneurship. He is a co-author of *Organizational Paradox* (Cambridge University Press, 2022) and the *Elgar Introduction to Designing Organizations* (Elgar, 2022). His papers have appeared in journals such as the *Academy of Management Review, Organization Studies, Harvard Business Review, Research in the Sociology of Organizations* and *Journal of Management Inquiry.*

Stewart R. Clegg is Professor at the University of Sydney in the School of Project Management and the John Grill Institute for Project Leadership, as well as a Distinguished Emeritus Professor at the University of Technology Sydney. He is recognized for his work in sociology, politics and power relations, organization studies and project management, to all of which he has contributed substantially over his career. His papers have appeared in journals such as *the Academy of Management Review, Organization Studies, Research in the Sociology of Organizations, Journal of Management Inquiry, Administrative Science Quarterly, Management Learning, Human Relations, Organization Science*, etc. His latest book is the second edition of *Frameworks of Power* (Sage).

Miguel Pina e Cunha is the Fundação Amélia de Mello chair professor at the Nova School of Business and Economics, NOVA University Lisbon (Portugal). His work deals with paradox, process (improvisation, serendipity), and positive approaches to work. He recently co-authored, with Stewart, *Paradoxes of Power and Leadership* (Routledge), recipient of the 2022 EURAM Best Book Award.

Acknowledgements

We are grateful to all of our colleagues who have helped us shape our thinking on organizational paradox over the years. The group that regularly meets in the EGOS paradox subtheme and AOM works as a real community and has influenced how we see and study paradoxes – we are indebted to them all. We want to thank particularly our friend Marco Berti for helping us sharpen our thinking and for his feedback.

At Sage, we are grateful to Kirsty Smy, our editor, and Rabia Barkatulla, Daniel Price and Charlotte Hegley for their patience, feedback and support in completing the book.

Institutionally, Medhanie acknowledges the financial support of the Wallander and Tom Hedelius Foundation at Handelsbanken (W17-0030) and Riksbankens Jubileumsfond (P19-0597:1). Miguel Cunha acknowledges support from Fundação para a Ciência e a Tecnologia (UID/ECO/00124/2019, UIDB/00124/2020 and Social Sciences DataLab, PINFRA/22209/2016), POR Lisboa and POR Norte (Social Sciences DataLab, PINFRA/22209/2016).

1

Introduction to Organizational Paradox

Paradox thinking does not offer simplistic solutions to a complex world. Nonetheless, it is because paradox is becoming part of the language of management and organizations that we have written this book. The book is intended to be used as additional reading to the main textbooks used in class. In addition, it is a volume of interest to both researchers and practitioners. The book can be used in organization and management undergraduate courses in areas such as organization design and organization change, as well as strategy, covering themes such as leadership, decision-making, negotiation, and organization change. For first-year Master's courses, it provides useful material on strategy that is suitable for both small and large classes. Students will be able to use the cases in each chapter to move between theory and practice.

One basic idea underpins the book. Typically, organizations and their members are confronted by competing demands. These are evident in persistent and interwoven tensions; for instance, between meeting social obligations and achieving business missions; between exploring new opportunities and exploiting those already made routine; between a propensity for change and one for stability (Gaim et al., 2022). These paradoxes are present, often implicitly, in organizational and everyday language. While ordinarily one or the other of the choices available is made by individuals and organizations, scholars have more recently shown the value of accommodating competing demands simultaneously, not merely tolerating them, but actively embracing them. Research frames this as a paradox (Miron-Spektor et al., 2018; Smith and Lewis, 2011).

As organizations grow more complex, they are increasingly characterized by paradoxes. The concept of a paradox, defined as 'persistent contradictions between interdependent elements' (Schad et al., 2016: 10), is now widely used to describe generalized organizational phenomena. Paradoxical tensions are normal and inherent, rather than irrational absurdities that need to be removed. Managing them is the key. As noted by Hill and Davis (2017: 107), 'sometimes you have to create tension to stimulate thinking, ideas, and innovation'.

Not all contradictions are paradoxes. Some are better viewed as trade-offs or dilemmas that impose clear-cut decisions. For example, Toyota's success with hybrids says little about its success in electric vehicles (EV). Toyota risks losing its edge with the Prius in the hybrid market, as it shifts to a fully electric car.[1] Will its buyers simply trade off hybrid for electric with little in the way of new sales? Will its proposed new subscription-based business model in which consumers will return the cars at the end of the subscription period, be successful in allaying fear about depreciation (Kondo & Fukuda, 2022)? Other contradictions may be paradoxical because choice is impossible (Berti and Cunha, 2023). Examples might include choosing between the tension of striving for stability or for change. Must they choose one or the other? Is the choice even a 'problem' if stability is an illusion in a world of processual change? As Parmenides (Hutchinson, 2020) recognised, one can never step in the same river twice because its flow means it is constantly changing; perhaps organizations, like rivers, are always in flow?

Engaging paradoxes may often be necessary, but it is neither easy nor is it always desirable to do so. For example, tackling grand challenges requires leaders capable of maintaining a balance with stakeholders' voices rather than resolving trade-offs in favour of either shareholders or stakeholders. The idea that, as in the case of 'shared value' (Porter and Kramer, 2011) 'you can grow the pie without encountering any trade-offs' (Kaplan, 2023: 4) may be appealing, but it is also often impossible. Making choices is always a matter of uncertainty and ambiguity. It is a bold claim to make that people and organizations need not make choices of an either/or nature, that they can try to engage both sides of a paradox to spark dynamic interactions enabling long-term organizational sustainability (Gaim and Wåhlin, 2016; Putnam et al., 2016).

Managers, despite being aware that they face paradoxes, may well lack insights into how to frame and address these effectively. Competing demands seem to require choices rather than the embrace of contradictions (Smith et al., 2016). We need to approach paradox with a measure of caution and realism: using paradox thinking does not provide a recipe for dealing with the world, so much as for seeing its features in a novel way. Paradox thinking admits that contradictions are normal, seeing them as inevitable facets of complex systems such as organizations; it does not assume that these contradictions are controllable. While paradoxes cannot be

---

[1] 'Toyota risks losing its Prius edge in the shift from hybrid to fully electric cars', *Financial Times*, 17 October 2022. In the meantime, the company promised a breakthrough: 'Toyota says solid-state battery breakthrough can halve cost and size', *Financial Times*, 4 July 2023. Available at: ft.com.

'tamed' (Cunha and Putnam, 2019), 'both/and' (Smith and Lewis, 2022) approaches offer a practical way of approaching paradoxes without constituting a panacea.

The book introduces readers to a basic understanding of paradoxes, their philosophical underpinnings and their construction *in practice* (Molecke et al., 2023). Our readers will become more confident about the paradoxes they might face in life and be better able to deal with them and the contexts in which they arise. These contexts are many; paradoxes mark key areas of contemporary life, including innovation, leadership, governance and sustainability, at different levels of analysis (individual, group, organization). As individuals, we face paradoxical choices every day. For instance, buyers of vehicles face a paradox: should they choose an electric platform or a combustion engine for personal mobility? Should they prioritize sustainability or convenience? Petrol may seem more expensive than solar-powered energy, but how far can they go on one battery charge? Petrol stations are widely available in most places, while at present, charging stations are not as plentiful. If you live in a city and rarely venture elsewhere, electric might work for you; however, if you live out on the prairies or in the bush, the distances and relative scarcity of charging stations may negate any desire to transition. While solar energy is free, the installation of panels, inverters and batteries is not: how should their cost be weighed against the cost of petrol? Ethically, we know that petrol is an unsustainable fuel in terms of the planet's health, while batteries pose problems regarding end-of-life recycling: which unsustainability should you opt for? Managers spend time crafting detailed plans, while doubting their real value (Chia and Mackay, 2023).

Managers strive to get things done, but they can only do so through other people. Paradoxically, other people often do not want to be told what to do, but asked what do they want to do: how can leadership both lead and not lead simultaneously to allow room for other views to be heard? One way is to tell people that they must speak up so that their views can be heard. Nonetheless, to do so is paradoxical: telling people that they *must* participate is not the best way to encourage genuine contributions. All it might generate is a sense of saying something – anything – to meet a quota of suggestions.

Why paradox?

Paradoxes abound. They are common in our personal lives and they intersect with the social world. Esther Perel, a relationship therapist, explains that we have two fundamental and contradictory needs in our relationships. These are for predictability and surprise, safety and adventure, permanence and novelty, making life potentially paradoxical. We crave the excitement of romantic adventures, but fear the consequences if our life partner discovers these adventures. We want to be unique and independent, but our collective behaviour is regulated, standardized and rendered predictable by tools such as clocks. Indeed, before people could afford to have wrist or pocket watches, and long before mobile phones, time was told by the clock towers typical of both mediaeval villages and industrial factory towns, while other tools, such as factory whistles, punctuated the working day, establishing the rhythm of life (see Figure 1.1).

Business managers are confronted with paradoxes. For instance, some organizations have their own unique tensions, such as family businesses, which have been described as a 'mass of contradictions'.[2] A recent survey confirmed that 'All stakeholders hold businesses accountable', which means that businesses are confronted with a multiplicity of expectations that they cannot satisfactorily integrate.[3] According to a Fortune commissioned survey, two-thirds of American adults believe that companies should have the objective of making the world a better place (Rigby, First, & O'Keeffe, 2023). But can a company make the world a better place without a profit?

Figure 1.1   The clocktower of CUF, Barreiro, Portugal (© Miguel Cunha)

Paradoxes mark global politics. If you are following the news about the Russian invasion of Ukraine from the US, UK and EU, you might notice your leaders struggling with the paradox of helping Ukraine to defeat Russia while trying to avoid direct confrontation with Russia (2022 onwards). For outside observers, who haven't been

---

[2]'The lure of the family business', *The Economist*, 8 April 2023, p. 58.

[3]The 2022 Edelman Trust Barometer. Available at: www.edelman.com/trust/2022-trust-barometer

directly affected by the war, the West's action might seem absurd. Even though they have been supplying Ukraine with considerable artillery and intelligence, they have so far been reluctant to provide certain weapons, such as F-111 jet planes that can reach far into Russia and its bases in occupied Ukraine. They do not want to risk provoking Russian escalation, possibly to nuclear weapons, which Putin intimates could be used. Their reluctance to engage, while extending some support, seems a little like trying to have their cake and eat it too. At the moment, as Professor Andre Spicer of Bayes Business School, noted, 'there is less to lose from continuing the support and more to lose by withdrawing the support' (Spicer, 2023), but how will those nations supporting Ukraine deal with the paradox as the war continues to unfold?

In a different domain, one of the hottest topics in tech, which captured the attention of millions, has been OpenAI's introduction of ChatGPT, launched in November 2022. ChatGPT showed the potential of AI, which can generate human-sounding answers to queries. It has amazed many with its facility, from composing poems to acing bar exams, to correcting coding errors. It can do all this and much more, producing plausible accounts. With such a potential also come issues of accuracy and the risk of manipulation and deception. As much as AI might improve efficiency, it is also spreading panic across sectors, including education. Hence, the paradox is that as actors attempt to support the development and deployment of something that could be helpful, they fear allowing its use, without providing a guardrail to avoid unintended consequences. There is no guardrail at present, and thus there is an evident paradox of optimism and scepticism, often in the same reactions to the new technology.

Paradoxes have, in summary, become ubiquitous in organizations. From being treated as anomalies, paradoxes have become the new normal (Gaim, 2017) for many reasons. The business context has changed: there are multiple pressures from multiple actors forcing organizations to move beyond unidimensional views in which only the bottom line mattered (Friedman, 1970). Competition has intensified where customers expect not only better, but also cheaper, products and services. In addition, paradoxes are more visible because of our increased understanding, as well as the tools, for dealing with them. Thus, given the push and pull factors, we envision that this book will equip you not only with an understanding of paradoxes, but also the tools that you need to deal with them effectively.

What is different?

As an introductory text, designed to supplement textbooks and compendia of journal articles, we will guide readers through paradox theory, covering peripherally conceptual exotica as well as ideas now incorporated in the mainstream. The book is written in an accessible way, using familiar cases, so that it can be easily used by students at both the graduate and undergraduate levels. It is designed as an exemplary introductory book for all those studying management and organization studies, organization behaviour and strategy, highlighting some of the paradoxes that can be encountered in these areas.

Topics include leadership, creativity, innovation, emotion, sustainability, coopetition (collaboration and competition), gender, culture, power and cognition – a range that makes the proposed book versatile. For MBA students and interested practitioners, it provides a succinct introduction to an increasingly popular practical approach.

How can the book help students?

Students sometimes expect easy answers and recipes that tend to stress rational linear thinking. In fact, they often want to know the best practices, seven steps and decision trees to follow. These envisage no tensions and paradoxes. Neat and tidy analytical worlds rarely align with complex practices. It may seem easier to ignore tensions between social and business missions, exploration and exploitation, change and stability. It may sound easier to think dualistically in terms of non-overlapping oppositions. In fact, a rationalist tradition tends to direct organization theory in the direction of a dichotomous thinking (Grimand et al., 2018). Despite this default approach, the complexity of the world is better considered from a duality perspective, one in which oppositions are mutually enabling (Farjoun, 2010). Organizations are increasingly being invited to 'embrace dynamic duality' (metaphorically, consider Figure 1.2). For example, Toyota moves slowly but takes big leaps; while it is hierarchical, it also gives employees freedom to push back (Nonaka and Takeuchi, 2021). Consider this example from strategy:

> The widely accepted distinction between the 'operational' and the 'strategic' is, in truth, arbitrary and any imagined separation is more a result of the influence of widely disseminated business school teaching and consultancy practices grounded in the convenience of a discipline-based teaching curriculum'. (Chia and Mackay, 2023: 8)

In terms of company practice, this dualistic orientation may result from the convenience of thinking of specialized business functions, such as marketing or finance.

When two opposite goals may be needed *how* can both be accomplished simultaneously? Enter paradox theory.

Consider the discussions of central management and organization studies topics, such as integrating sustainability into teaching, and how it poses paradoxical issues. Students need to learn not only what being sustainable means analytically. While understanding the notion of a circular economy is important, so also is knowing what to do *to be sustainable in practice*. How to do more with less is a paradox that is central to answering that question.

The book provides foundations for exploring paradoxical ways of thinking and doing. Our aim is engaging readers' understanding of the nature of competing demands, as well as the contexts in which they arise (for example, in innovation, leadership, governance and sustainability), as well as how to deal with them. The book is designed to supplement the easy rationalities of most textbooks.

Figure 1.2   Dynamic duality in nature: Ngorongoro, Tanzania (© Miguel Cunha)

How to read the book

We are scholars writing for novices interested in organizational paradoxes. Depending on what you want to get out of your reading, the book can be read in different ways. If a basic understanding of paradoxes and how they are managed is your interest, focus on Chapters 2 and 5. If you want a more comprehensive understanding of paradoxes, add Chapters 6 and 7. If you want to explore areas for research, focus on Chapters 4, 6 and 8. If it is the challenges and unintended consequences of paradoxes that interest you, focus on Chapter 7.

How to use the book

Educators can use the book in different ways. We present a few possibilities below:

- **Strategy** How can organizations explore new possibilities and exploit existing capabilities? How can leaders manage for today and tomorrow? How can managers build upon the past while leaving the past behind to create the future?
- **Organizational change** How can managers balance change and stability? How can organizations change while still ensuring continuity? How can managers change to ensure that everything remains the same?

- **Organizational design** How can managers maintain control *and* flexibility? How can organizations compete *and* collaborate simultaneously? How can organization designs be structured so that they do not ossify processes?
- **Leadership** How can managers engage in control to ensure efficiency and delegation to empower their followers? How can followers also be leaders?

To connect theory with practice, we have used a number of illustrative cases throughout the book. Some of the cases are presented in separate boxes to maintain our argument and the general flow of the book. They are used only as illustrations and imply neither criticism nor endorsement of the companies or individuals in these cases. Things change and what might have seemed positive at one time may not be so in future; what seems negative today might become positive tomorrow. Mismanagement and decline might be sharply turned into excellence. We endorse no product, organization or people.

Additionally, it is important to note that we do not advocate paradox as superior to alternative approaches to management and organization. When we present paradox as a way of seeing, it does not exclude other ways of seeing. Linear models have their uses. For example, change management models such as John Kotter's eight steps are helpful for acting in and on the world. Paradox perspectives provide a way of seeing and being in the world rather than a straightforward manual for its change, as does Kotter's approach (Kotter, 2012). Applying Kotter can produce change through the 'aspirational vision' (Bednarek and Smith, 2023) of change programmes, which have an inspiring and energizing idealistic component. Nonetheless, these can create paradoxes: change programmes often lead to resistance. The more things seem to change, the more they really do stay much the same, just with an added layer of cynicism on the part of those being asked to change. When change programmes appear to be a constant cycle, cynicism frequently prevails. Searching for dynamic equilibrium often produces conflict and disequilibrium (Benson, 1977).

2

What Is (not) a Paradox?

This chapter will start by introducing the reader to the notion of paradox. It will centre on paradoxes and how they differ from related concepts, such as dilemmas and trade-offs. We begin with paradoxes that individuals face in their everyday lives. Then we move on to paradoxes that exist in organizational life. We will show how problematization is important. Do you see a competing demand as a dilemma? Might it better be seen as a paradox? How to avoid miscategorization that can be potentially ambiguous? We will consider how competing demands are problematized and what this means for both theory and practice.

Philosophers, psychologists and sociologists have all viewed human existence as paradoxical. Lewis (2000: 760) noted that paradox is used to describe 'conflicting demands, opposing perspectives, or seemingly illogical findings'. In organizational settings, paradoxes result from interdependent contradictions that persist as often puzzling yet unavoidable aspects of organized life (Schad et al., 2016). Persistent paradoxes often seem to defy organizational logic (Berti, 2021). Despite all of management's efforts in striving to make organizations more rational, paradoxes remain a pervasive feature of organizing. Are paradoxical attributes a sign of dysfunction and inefficiency? Not necessarily – they may be seen as reflections of complex contemporary organization.

Paradoxes can be conceptually challenging and ambiguous. Sometimes they are confused with adjacent but distinct concepts. Generally, the term 'paradox' is used to label phenomena that seem puzzling, counter-intuitive, even absurd. Often, what are paradoxes may be labelled as dilemmas or trade-offs (Gaim et al., 2018). Top management may want to treat competing demands as paradoxes, but those who have to accommodate conflicting demands in practice, lower down the hierarchy, may see these as trade-offs or dilemmas. When this happens, there is a gap created between *saying* and *doing* (Gaim et al., 2021). The 'say/do gap' refers to the discrepancy between what is said and what is done, what is prescribed and what is practised. Think about equal opportunity commitments (Täuber, 2019). They can apply to us as individuals, consumers, employees and business managers. Entire organizations, public and private, may be held accountable to their terms. Still, #MeToo flourished in the midst of all the talk and text dedicated to respectful gender relations and the importance of diversity. Were organization members dealing with paradox when it arose? Were they paying cynical lip service or were they just blind? Does #MeToo signify a saying/doing gap (Child, 2020)? Commonly, paradoxes are regarded as presenting a choice between two seemingly irreconcilable options – so that is where we will start.

Problematizing competing demands

The frame through which we see a problem shapes how we deal with it. As Gaim et al. (2018: 14) note, 'problems never announce themselves as such; they must be problematized and their problematization depends on being able to read the signs correctly'. Sparr et al. (2022) also note that if we change the way we look at things, the things we look at change. What is seen depends on 'ways of seeing' (Berger, 1972). Think of choices and how they can be seen. Some examples might help. Let's consider architects' work.

An architect's everyday work might involve many decisions. Some will relate to form and function; some will articulate aesthetic passion, while others will demand discipline. A senior architect responsible for the office might have to choose between a lucrative project that ensures continuity of the office (focus on commercial objective) or a project that places the office in a prestigious architectural design magazine (focus on aesthetics). While the latter will be highly prized by other architects, potential clients at large will probably never know about the award (Gaim, 2018; Gaim et al., 2022). Similarly, a manager of a large firm might be faced with competing demands: What is to be done today and what should be done tomorrow? Maximize profit or improve social welfare? Explore new ideas or exploit existing knowledge (Smith, 2014)?

When you face competing demands, the tension that follows can trigger different emotions. For some, they experience tension as 'stress, anxiety, discomfort, or tightness in making choices, responding to, and moving forward' (Putnam et al., 2016: 71). For others, the tension can be a source of excitement, a new opportunity, an occasion for creativity or even a fun part of business as it evolves (Beech et al., 2004; Cunha et al., 2023c).

People in organizations feeling tension as a result of competing demands do so not only emotionally (Pradies, 2023) but also cognitively (Miron-Spektor et al., 2011). Within the bounds of organizational resources and routines, they will struggle to make sense of the tension (Berti and Simpson, 2021; Berti et al., 2021).

Routines may be paradoxically ever changing or never changing patterns of interaction (Pentland et al., 2011). Given all the competing demands faced by individuals, teams and organizations, they may all problematize the resulting tensions differently. Thus, tension might be seen as dilemmas, trade-offs or paradoxes.

Dilemmas denote the 'simultaneous presence of two equally (un)desirable goals/requirements that cannot be achieved simultaneously' (Putnam et al., 2016: 73). When competing demands are problematized as dilemmas, choice of one at the expense of the other can be considered a deliberate strategy. Having both is neither possible nor desirable. When car manufacturers have to accommodate emissions standards, efficiency and performance demands, some make different choices. For example, BMW met emissions standards by reducing fuel efficiency, which ultimately led them to increase the price of their cars to meet the costs of a solution to the new problem of fuel inefficiency that they had created. Yet, efficiency or the price of vehicles might not be the priority of all firms. When a choice is forced, it might lead to a disastrous outcome, as is evident in the VW emissions scandal. Trying to be all things at once, it claimed to produce fast, cheap and clean vehicles (Gaim et al., 2021).

As illustrated by the collapse of FTX and other organizations (Box 2.1), too much focus on one goal at the expense of another might lead to an undesirable outcome.

Box 2.1   The Icarus paradox

Nokia, the cell phone king

In 2007, Nokia had 900 million users, which gave the company a market supremacy that led Forbes magazine to ask, 'Can anyone catch the cell phone king?'. That year, Apple launched the iPhone.[1]

The collapse of FTX

By the end of 2022, one of the most talked about business stories was the collapse of an industry giant FTX and the arrest of its founder, Sam Bankman-Fried, who founded FTX in 2019 to become a major player in the cryptocurrency industry. In November 2022, an abrupt surge of customer withdrawals was sparked by reports of unstable finances. Soon after the report, FTX was forced to declare bankruptcy. Before it went bankrupt, FTX operated a cryptocurrency exchange, with the founder acquiring an estimated net worth of US $26 billion before being sentenced to 25 years in jail for fraud in 2024.

(Continued)

[1]McGee, P., 'How Apple tied its fortunes to China', *Financial Times*, 18 January 2023, p. 17.

SVB

The Silicon Valley Bank became world famous in 2023 when it collapsed. The bank was modern and agile, but in a negative way. It is said to have promoted a culture of empathy and innovation at the expense of risk management. Its top managers, as the bank grew, became increasingly focused on social issues. 'I almost felt like I was at work on a college campus,' a former executive pointed out, remembering the weekly TED talks on social issues.[2]

In summary

The three cases above are useful to explain what is called the Icarus paradox, where individuals achieve initial success but subsequently fail spectacularly. Daedalus and Icarus are characters in Greek mythology. Daedalus, a skilled craftsman and inventor, was imprisoned on the island of Crete by King Minos. To escape, he fashioned two pairs of wings out of wax and feathers for himself and his son, Icarus. He warned his son not to fly too close to the sun, but Icarus became carried away and did fly too close, causing the wax on his wings to melt so that he plummeted into the sea and drowned.

The story of Daedalus and Icarus is often used as a cautionary tale about the dangers of overreaching and disregarding caution by focusing on short-terms gain at the expense of long-term survival. This conundrum is not limited to business. We see it in politics as well, where leaders become too focused on maintaining power and end up neglecting the needs and concerns of their constituents, leading to a decline in popularity and support.

Trade-offs involve facing competing demands as a problem to be solved by optimizing (Berti and Cunha, 2023). In a trade-off, more of one thing means less of other things (Gaim et al., 2018). For example, in combustion engine design, engineers increase performance for which customers must pay more. In major infrastructure projects, engineers and architects, confronted with the tension between form and function, might arrive at a mutually acceptable outcome (Gaim, 2018). Or they might not: the story of the construction of the Sydney Opera House was a constant struggle between the architects' sense of aesthetics and the engineers' sense of function (Gaim et al., 2022). Such a situation is especially likely to arise in cases where there is power symmetry between two parties, such that one party can't impose its will on the other (Berti and Cunha, 2023).

Trade-offs imply competing demands that are mutually exclusive, where gains for one necessitate a proportional sacrifice on the part of the other (Berti and Cunha, 2023). The more I concede to you, the less I have and vice versa. It is what is called a zero-sum game. When juggling work and life, the practical decision is 'how much time, energy and effort go into one domain versus the other' (Putnam et al., 2014: 416).

---

[2]Kinder, T. and Gara, A., 'Collapse casts light on SVB culture and strategy', *Financial Times*, 17 March 2023, p. 9.

Box 2.2   Muay Thai vs Taekwondo

In martial arts, individuals specialize in different styles. The choice of certain styles – e.g. Muay Thai or Taekwondo – comes with certain choices and decisions in terms of *speed* and *strength*. Both styles utilize kicking as a key element of their techniques, but in different ways.

Muay Thai is known for its powerful striking techniques and is designed to be powerful, the goal being to knock out an opponent or cause significant damage. Taekwondo, on the other hand, is known for its fast, high kicks, and jumping and spinning kicks. Taekwondo kicks are typically designed to be precise and fast, with the goal of scoring points in competition. Although having both a powerful and fast kick may be desirable, a choice to specialize on one or other style means that individuals must make a choice to focus on either power or speed.

The example in Box 2.2 exemplifies a typical trade-off. When confronted with competing demands, it is rarely the case to confront a strict either/or, where the presence of one thing implies the absence of another. Choosing Muay Thai or Taekwondo doesn't mean that speed and strength are either present or absent. Both strength and speed will be present, but the focus of one's training will be geared towards one at the expense of the other. The same is true for those who compete in bodybuilding vs those who compete in the world's strongman competitions.

We make trade-offs all the time. You have probably made a trade-off today during breakfast or lunch between what is convenient and healthy. Or, if you have flown recently, choosing between booking either more affordable or fast/comfortable options.

Paradox denotes 'persistent contradictions between interdependent elements' (Schad et al., 2016: 10). The tension between independent and contradictory demands is persistent because it is impossible to take sides. Departing from the work of a German social scientist, Berti and Cunha (2023) develop the ideas of Niklas Luhmann on 'undecidability', meaning 'the impossibility to split, or to assimilate an entity to either side of a dichotomy or opposition' to demonstrate that in such a situation, an either/or solution is not sustainable (see also Box 2.4). Under certain conditions, synergy might be possible, but an incorrect or inappropriate choice will lead to forced choice or pragmatic paradox (Berti and Cunha, 2023; Berti and Simpson, 2021). One can end up saying one thing while knowingly doing the opposite to that which is claimed (Gaim et al., 2021).

Box 2.3   Elon Musk, Twitter and content moderation

After the chaotic takeover of Twitter by Elon Musk, the issue of content moderation has taken central stage. Although Musk, a self-proclaimed 'free speech absolutist', aimed at creating a maximally trusted and broadly inclusive platform, he ended up

(Continued)

banning users (including journalists) against his own convictions (later reversing the decision). Content moderation on social media involves making difficult decisions about what content should be allowed and what should be removed from the platform. Such a consequential decision also involves multiple paradoxes.

First, freedom of speech vs hate speech, which involves a difficult to manage paradox because in a polarized political space, what constitutes hate speech is not easy to determine. Much of it may be 'dog-whistling', appearing to be one thing in reality, while it is surreptitiously sending another message that those attuned to hearing it will understand all too well. Thus, what content should be allowed, and which should be removed, as well as the policies that govern such decisions, is not easy to develop and implement.

Second, there is the matter of consistency vs fairness in applying content moderation policies, particularly when dealing with a large volume of content. A policy that misses either side of the paradox will raise issues of bias and unequal treatment of users – a recipe for disaster if such users have a strong base.

Third, transparency vs accountability, which occurs where Twitter (now rebranded as 'X') faces pressure to be transparent about its content moderation policies and decisions, while also maintaining the privacy of users. Elon Musk, in one of his interviews before finalizing the acquisition said, 'it should be clear that there is no behind-the-scenes manipulation either algorithmically or manually'. He then made the algorithm open source. Since an algorithm is an artefact made by humans, there should be accountability when such moderation leads to bias, error or harm. For instance, face recognition software is standardized on white European sources of appearance, not those of Africans or Asians, sometimes with regrettable results.[3]

On top of how CEOs want to run their companies, there are legal and regularity requirements regarding privacy and hate speech, for example. As a business entity, there are also user expectations. These can be as diverse as they are polarized, which makes any decision about content moderation consequential. Such decisions will affect both user acquisition and advertising, which is the business side of X. Thus, would Musk's absolutist free speech stance push current users out and invite unhinged users into what they might consider (un)regulated space? Will businesses be happy to use the platform to advertise if new moderations are deemed too unregulated? Recently, Disney and other big firms stopped advertising on X because it allowed content they consider inappropriate. For Elon Musk, will what he does on X affect the other businesses that he runs?

Dialectics: Scholars of organization have also explored dialectical change (Clegg and Cunha, 2018). In this case, tensions between contradictory elements exist not as push–pulls in a state of dynamic equilibrium, as the mainstream organizational paradox theory view (Smith and Lewis, 2011); rather they are seen as unstable forces that produce change. In a dialectical view, these tensions between forces – call

---

[3]See: www.privacycompliancehub.com/gdpr-resources/10-reasons-to-be-concerned-about-facial-recognition-technology/

them thesis vs antithesis – sometimes generate a synthesis that transcends both (Clegg et al., 2002). Dialectics, in contrast with mainstream paradox views, does not assume some sort of stability. On the contrary, the social world has an element of conflict that creates instability and change.

A dialectical view emphasizes the role of power and political conflict in organizations and society (Farjoun, 2019). The management of paradoxical tensions in this case is not only a matter of finding synergies, but also managing political conflict and process. Accordingly, paradox management is not only a matter of balance, but also an outcome of organizational politics (Ashforth and Reingen, 2014). Paradoxes can become embedded in circuits of power relations (Clegg, 2023) that frame how they are expressed. People may end up accepting paradoxical absurdities as normal because they do not have the power to counter the absurdity or because, where they can exercise power, they accept an element of absurdity in life, something that happens when leaders declare their commitment to goals and courses of action that they know are impossible to achieve (Newark, 2018).

Box 2.4   Paradox and the Gorgons

Niklas Luhmann's (2018) approach to paradox suggests that all decisions are paradoxical. This is because decisions that are not obvious make salient the alternative, the path that one decides not to take. Thus, decisions force the decision-makers to show their audiences that there are valid alternatives to the choice they made, while simultaneously persuading them that these options are not actual alternatives. Therefore, staring at the contradiction contained in decisions recalls the mythical Gorgons of Ancient Greek legend (Seidl et al., 2021). These three sisters, whose hair was made of living, venomous snakes, turned those who looked at them into stone. Two of them, Stheno and Euryale, were immortal, but that was not the case for Medusa, who was slain by Perseus, hero and demi-god.

Staring at paradox, akin to staring at the Gorgons, is paralysing. For this reason, paradoxes should be made latent, a process that Luhmann calls 'deparadoxization', displacing paradoxes to places that make them less problematic or concealing them, moving them out of sight. The paradoxes of decision are obscured in the process, with decision-makers hoping that the decision will not be dissected and the alternatives revisited and reconsidered. Attributing a decision to collectives, as well as making it partially incomprehensible, helps to keep paradoxes concealed.

Often actors decide automatically, following instinct or habit. Observers become paralysed by attempting to make rational sense of actions that lack reason. However, the impossibility of rationally deciding a course of action has important consequences in modern organizations. Actions undertaken in bureaucracies, the nub of modern organizations, are increasingly justified as the most effective and technically rational (Weber, 1978). Otherwise, why would they exist? Such logic can lead to disasters such as the Australian Robodebt scandal (Braithwaite, 2020) or the British Post Office's (Christie, 2020) pursuit of sub-postmasters erroneously thought to be fraudulent. In both cases, misplaced faith in technical rationality was the fundamental error.

Visualizing competing demands

The language (Keller and Tian, 2021), metaphors and symbols (see Figure 2.1) that people use to articulate and delimit a problem in an organizational capacity informs how they deal with it. Keller and Tian (2021: 101–2) note that 'language is not only a tool that we use to communicate with others, but also a tool that we use to think about the world we live in [...] how we experience paradox is therefore inextricably tied to the language we chose to make sense of and to construe our experience'. There are moments in which our everyday language opens windows on the paradoxical nature of organizational life. Paradoxical language includes expressions such as 'friendly fire' (Snook, 2011), 'creative destruction' (Elliott, 1980) or 'structured chaos' (Quinn, 1985).

It is not only words that can have paradoxical effects. In a recent work, Pradies et al. (2023) explored the figurative materialization of how paradoxes were visually represented. Different visuals and metaphors have been used in theoretically different ways. Not only do visuals and metaphors orient organizational actors' attention as a way of problematizing relations, but they also serve as communication devices and sources of inspiration. They can help us to see more than is obviously apparent. Visuals and metaphors can reveal what text alone cannot do, and some people will gain more understanding from visuals and metaphors than from text alone.

Tensions or the push–pull force that results from facing competing demands can be portrayed by a stretched rubber band, which in its simplest form describes 'tensions that emerge due to the impact of opposing physical forces' (Rosales et al., 2022: 9). As Putnam et al. (2014: 416) put it, tensions focus on the ways that opposite concepts or behaviours push and pull against one another, rebounding as they do so. Cognitive and emotional efforts can be pulled and pushed by contradictory forces (Rosales et al., 2022: 9). Like a rubber band, they are stretched in different directions: 'individuals often treat the activities of work and life as pushing and pulling against each other, which can produce the tensions' (Putnam et al., 2014: 432). Similarly, Gümüsay et al. (2020) use the notion of elasticity (elastic hybridity, to be exact) in their study of an Islamic bank as a hybrid organization that attends to competing logics through iteration. The authors note: 'metaphorically speaking, it renders the hybrid capable of *institutionally bending without organizationally breaking*' (Gümüsay et al., 2020: 126).

Visually, *dilemmas* are often represented as a fork in the road (Figure 2.1) where you must make a choice between two paths. Dilemmas imply that these competing demands are mutually exclusive; choosing one prevents you from selecting the other. Thus, if one person sees a tension as a dilemma, it means that one path leads to one outcome, while another person might see it as leading to a different outcome. Thus, as in the culmination of tug of war, one has to give in, either voluntarily or as a result of the opposing force (Berti and Cunha, 2023).

Trade-offs are usually portrayed by a pendulum swinging back and forth, in search of optimal resolution at rest. When competing demands are portrayed as trade-offs, there is a quest to find a middle ground in which each party will give up some of their initial demands so that they reach a solution that is acceptable to all. With a trade-off, the back and forth in the pendulum implies a compromise. When both parties find a middle ground that is sufficiently mutually satisfactory to both parties, they come to an agreement – a place in which they rest their competing demands – without necessarily finding a mutually beneficial outcome.

- **Forked path.** This symbolizes the tension between two demands, where a decision must be made at the intersection.

- **Balancing scales.** This symbolizes the quest for equilibrium between two choices. An imbalance indicates the relative weight, importance, or intensity given to each. The fulcrum, where the two forces balance, represents a point of decision or compromise between the two demands.

- **Balancing on a tightrope.** This symbolizes the delicate act of managing competing demands. A slight shift in the process can have a significant consequence.

- **Rubber band.** This symbolizes a tug of war, with the pushing and pulling against each other of competing demands. Stretching the rubber band signifies the capacity to adapt to pressure, while too much of it could risk a potential snap.

- **Juggling.** This symbolizes the act of managing multiple demands simultaneously, with each ball representing a priority. The act of juggling implies that all demands are in motion, and organizational members must keep them afloat.

- **Yin-Yang.** This symbolizes the harmony of opposing demands. Each half signifies a different demand with an element of the other.

- **Mule.** As a blend of a female horse and a male donkey, this symbolizes a hybrid of complementary traits and strengths.

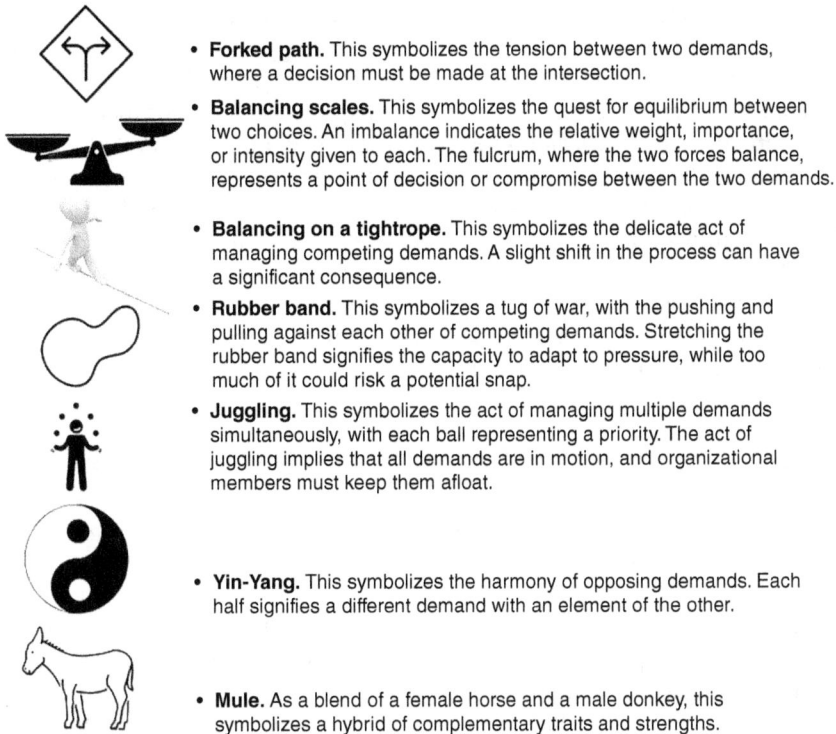

Figure 2.1 Visualizing competing demands

Paradoxes are often visually portrayed using the yin–yang symbol, from ancient Chinese philosophy (Li, 2016), which is used to represent the idea that things exist both as opposing and interconnected forces. These are forces that exist in a combination of synergy and trade-off (Li, 2016). The coexistence of synergies and trade offs is indicative of the dynamism of paradox. In addition, it captures the difficulty of maintaining equilibrium as well as the complexity and nuance of the relationship between intertwined opposites, such as organizing dualities of the exploration–exploitation type (Li et al., 2023; Zhou et al., 2023). How much should an organization exploit what it already knows, against how much it should master what it does not know?

To make matters more complicated, equilibrium, being dynamic, is not a 50–50 balance between forces. In some cases, equilibrium is maintained by emphasizing the element of tradition. Centuries-old organizations are distinctive because of their tradition. This is because, to keep traditions appearing the same, they must adapt significantly as the world around them changes. In other words, balance is a delicate process: it should be managed with care.

The boundaries separating yin and yang highlight their distinctions while the external boundary integrates the overall system, representing the synergies between the two (Smith and Lewis, 2011: 386). As illustrated by Spencer-Rodgers et al. (2010: 297–8), the outer circle can be seen to capture the concept of context, holistic thinking and the emphasis on the big picture. In addition, the symbol also represents change. Contradiction is represented by the black-and-white dots: every element in the universe is seen to contain something of its opposite (see Peng and Nisbett, 1999). The idea is captured in a lyric such as 'There is a thin line between love and hate' (Poindexter et al., 1971). Many people experience what is called a 'love–hate relationship', in which the feelings for each other are complicated and often extreme.

In addition to the above, there are other metaphors used to portray tension and the pursuit of balancing or accommodating competing demands. For example, Smith and Lewis (2022) use balancing on a tightrope to portray competing demands, and what it means to live with tensions and paradoxes. In relation to work–life balance, *juggling* is also used to describe multiple tasks that require individuals' simultaneous attention. The image of juggling, when describing work–life balance, portrays managing multiple responsibilities at the same time, trying to keep all the 'balls' in the air without dropping any of them.

Paradoxes' multiple manifestations: levels of analysis

Paradox can be manifested at multiple levels of analysis. Individual level paradoxes occur in specific contexts, taking place time and again. Meta-paradoxes are less individual and context specific.

Individual level paradoxes: Paradoxes are manifest at the individual level. Each one of us strives to be unique as an individual while, at the same time, belonging to several collectives. Individuals are in a constant process of vacillation between uniting with others (socialization) and disbanding from these associations (individuation). In teams, for instance, we are always involved in a process of identity differentiation and maintenance (Weick, 1969). More generally, we play multiple roles as members of a family and a professional organization. These roles introduce tensions. For example, investing in work to provide for our families may deplete them of needed attention. If some balance gets lost, even justifications ('I'm working hard to provide my kids the best possible education') will be insufficient to prevent tension and conflict (Hewlett and Luce, 2006). People are expected to find a calling and do what they love to do, but the potential exploitation involved in this equation is undeniable (Dobrow et al., 2023).

In organizations, managers are expected to complement the power of position with personal authority, to command both compliant obedience and honourable respect, even if making difficult demands. Leadership work has always been riddled with paradoxes. Consider the following analysis:

> If an hierarchy is to be maintained, it must be continuously re-established by the person above's sending acceptable orders to the person below (in Barnard's language, orders must be within the zone of indifference for subordinates). (Weick, 1969: 5)

Leadership exists in a state of tension. Leaders need hard skills (literacy, numeracy, coding) as well as practical, soft skills (clear communication, putting others at ease). Leaders must be able to accept and accommodate followers' motives and expectations, without which they lack legitimacy to lead. On the other hand, they need to influence the collective will, without which there is no leadership (Weick, 1969).

Leadership in democratic systems has a dual challenge: it cannot distance itself too much from the will of the people, while leaders must be able to shape this will in the pursuit of some higher motives that are, perhaps, invisible to the multitude in the short run. These leaders accommodate and embody their political organizations and shape them at the same time in a permanent dialectic. The balance is one of story-telling that connects the past with a desired future, and spells out the direction to be followed to realize a future that a majority can be persuaded to accept. When this balance fails, collective organization will either succumb to the will of an autocrat, leading regardless of the will of the majority, or by spineless representatives lacking the capacity to give sense to the future and to lead its enactment.

In recent times, leadership prototypes have been changing from a logic of *power over* (command and control) to a logic of *power with* (coaching, empowerment). Changes in work and technology facilitated the shift. As organizations became more professionalized, autonomously professional people (for example, doctors or lawyers) were employed in increasing numbers. Professional expertise is highly legitimated (Petriglieri et al., 2019), which invests professionals with more authority than less professionalized people.

The more professionalized the organization, the less hierarchical its organizational contexts will tend to be (Lee and Edmondson, 2017). Leadership is changing from control vested in an apex of control. Leaders are now supposed to display tough love (Gu et al., 2020), express servant leadership styles (Van Dierendonck, 2011) and show determination while acknowledging the importance of hesitancy (Bathurst and Cheng, 2023). In this new paradigm, even hereditary rulers present themselves as servants of the people (Sousa et al., 2022). These servant leaders are expected to express a mix of idealism and pragmatism (March and Weil, 2009); as coaches, they perform multiple roles, with contradictory demands (Milner et al., 2022). They are encouraged to be authentic and positive. Positivity and authenticity are paradoxical (Cunha et al., 2021a) because they combine opposites: to be authentic implies a measure of restraint and awareness (Kets de Vries, 2017) whereas being positive involves enthusiasm to motivate rather than restraint to be cool (Cunha et al., 2022). Being positive does not mean the absence of the negative, which is a practical impossibility. In short, leaders are confronted with many paradoxes that they have to engage. It has been claimed that 'leaders are increasingly calling for more paradoxical approaches to address complex organizational phenomena' (Bednarek and Smith, 2023: 4), including inequality and sustainability.

Subordinates, represented as collaborators, are expected to bring their 'entire self' to work. More than cogs in the organizational machine, they are encouraged to have agency. Their upward influence is viewed as legitimate, at least in theory in the most progressive organizations. They sometimes exert their influence via voice (speaking up), by tempered resistance or even through employee activism. These approaches can be received with more or less an open organizational embrace. Sometimes specific people's voice is received differentially, even where equality constitutes a formal legitimate value (Cunha et al., 2019), which is another paradox.

In their study of digital workplaces, Kokshagina and Schneider (2023) saw individual level paradoxes that required adjusting behaviour to deal with tensions. For example, regarding digitalization, people expect customer-based solutions but do not want to share their personal data (Majchrzak et al., 2023). Organizations also confront their contradictions: more organizations are now using a 'self-service' software model, in which employees sort things like travel and expenses through insourced portals in the name of empowerment and efficiency. Doing this creates 'shadow work', whose impacts on productivity are not acknowledged. At the end, as the *Financial Times*'s Sarah O'Connor put it, 'we are all secretaries now'.[4] As such, gains in one dimension may correspond to bigger losses in another dimension.

Paradox theory contributes to explaining the hybrid nature of organizations, including social organization as well as business firms or state organizations. In organizations that are hybrid, managing implies being able to think and lead paradoxically (Smith and Cunha, 2020). One example of paradoxical tensions was seen in a case study of 4AD, the record company of bands such as the Pixies and the Cocteau Twins. Cunha et al. (2019), researching the leadership of the label, plotted a tension between aesthetic purpose and the need for profit, required to maintain the aesthetics. Balancing the two was a perpetual tension for the founder.

In the emerging digital workplace, individuals face paradox as they navigate flexibility and accessibility (Kokshagina and Schneider, 2022). While there are efficacy and autonomy gains from digitally working from home, the efficiency gained through digital interaction leads to stresses. Working online is tiring and intensive. Moreover, the autonomy gained through digital interaction means being constantly ready to react immediately to whatever digital stimuli you are exposed.

In another case, architects were seen to navigate between passion (what they wanted to do) and discipline (what they had to do) (Gaim et al., 2019) in their day-to-day work, especially when there were limited resources, such as billable hours. For an architect working on a personally interesting project, accommodating passion and discipline meant making decisions as to whether to spend more time on the personal project during off work hours or to compromise by doing other, less interesting but more remunerative, projects.

Group level paradoxes: Teams are normally presented as units in which the power of diversity can be harnessed. Different people are thought to bring diverse talents which, when put together, can create a number of valued outputs, including innovation as well as a sense of belonging. Of course, in practice, things can differ. Even talented individuals in a team may *not* develop positive outcomes because the teamwork is beset by tensions of one sort or another. There are sometimes factions within a team that turn a group of talented individuals into a unit in which people neutralize one another (Anand and Barsoux, 2023).

In sports teams, a constellation of stars sometimes becomes a self-sabotaging team as each seeks to shine to the detriment of team discipline. As Smith and Berg (1987) explored, paradoxes matter at the group level where the need for individual difference and collective cohesion is present. The need to be different and similar at the same time often occurs in a typical team. An excessive emphasis on difference will tear the group apart, while excess collective pressure will lead to groupthink (Janis, 1983), where everyone is conforming to a collective logic by sharing and

---

[4]O'Connor, S., 'We are all secretaries now', *Financial Times*, 28 March 2023, p. 17. Available at: www.ft.com/content/e30e51b5-2d57-430e-a829-5965313c6c6b

self-censoring specific views. Inward-looking teams may become isolated and find it difficult to communicate with other teams.

Teams thrive on the capacity to combine a measure of psychological safety, the perception of the team as a safe space, with an emphasis on accountability, to avoid complacency (Edmondson, 1999, 2018). As explained by Toto Wolff, the leader of the Mercedes F1 team, wins should be treated the same way as losses, as opportunities to learn. For this to happen, analysing mistakes should occur without assigning blame for fault (Elberse, 2022) but as opportunities for learning. This balance can be easier said than done, especially in sectors in which the consequences of errors may be catastrophic, such as medical practice (Muethel et al., 2023). For this reason, physicians struggle to eliminate error *and* to embrace error to learn positively from it, a difficult balancing act (Cunha et al., 2024; Lei and Naveh, 2019).

To further complicate the process, psychological safety doesn't mean that you can say what you like. Everything has consequences. To stimulate and support good conversations, psychological safety must involve a 'balance of advocacy and inquiry'.[5] In some moments, organizations may benefit from the presence of experts in 'insultancy', professional critics that air problems everybody knows exist but nobody wants to own.[6] Sometimes they need, in other words, to play the role of a *wise jester* (Clegg et al., 2022). Teams, in summary, benefit from the capacity to articulate tensions inherent to teamwork. While it is often said by motivational speakers that there is no I in team, people may strive to shine in their individual contributions but also accept the rules of the team game; as de Rond (2012) put it, 'there is an I in team'. Teams, in summary, are paradoxical social units (Silva et al., 2014).

Group members have to navigate the contradictions that result when they seek to both excel and belong, to become more enmeshed and more outstanding (Smith and Berg, 1987). The paradox of belonging (see Chapter 3) is visible at a group level especially when there are polar differences among members. For example, groups that identify with competing demands can be polarized in intractable turf wars (Schad et al., 2016). The politics of us/them or we/they is a powerful tendency.

On the flip side, paradox at group levels, when managed properly, can lead to team creativity. In what is termed as 'the innovation paradox' two forces might be at play. Idea generation, requiring 'out-of-the-box thinking, exploration, risk taking, and tolerance of mistakes' must co-exist with 'idea implementation', which requires promoting an idea through accepted channels, by prototyping, testing and integrating innovation in existing ways of doing things (Miron-Spektor et al., 2011: 741).

Organizational level paradoxes: Paradoxes can be manifested at an organizational level. Organizations are expected to explore and exploit (March, 1991), or to express ambidexterity (Raisch et al., 2009; Visnjic et al., 2022). While they need to appear as competent in planning, they also need to improvise (Cunha et al., 1999) to be different from the competition, but not so different as not to relate to what competitors do. Organizations need to find a space of optimal distinctiveness (Zhao

---

[5]Hill, A., 'The art of encouraging teams to be more open'. *Financial Times*, 13 February 2023, p. 12. Available at: www.ft.com/content/5d544a25-d7dc-41ad-8b42-fe92406d25d7

[6]Balch, O., 'CEO whisperers: Who do bosses turn to in their hours of need?', *Financial Times*, 20 February 2023, p. 14. Available at: www.ft.com/content/e24f8965-6848-4f66-96d5-e39674a61cb3

and Glynn, 2022) but also to beware of too much difference. Organizations that are able to develop cultures that benefit from embracing competing values of cooperation, competition, following rules and breaking them through innovation are seen to flourish (Cameron et al., 2022). An excess of emphasis on any one of these elements, however, may damage an organization:

- An excess of a competitive orientation may intoxicate the organization with an obsession with goals, as happened in the Wells Fargo Bank (Ordóñez et al., 2009). In this bank, people committed fraud, opening unwanted accounts, in order to reach managerial objectives (Independent Directors of the Board of Wells Fargo & Company, 2017).
- Too many rules create coercive bureaucracies (Adler and Borys, 1996). These are often found in state organizations, where rules prevail over mission. In the higher education sector, faculty are often required to conduct 'box-ticking tasks' (Delucchi et al., 2021) that are meaningless in terms of education and research. People become tangled 'up in tasks that take them away from the work they want to do, like to do and were hired to do'.[7]
- Too much cooperation creates a cozy family feeling, with an element of complacency (Edmondson, 2018).
- Innovation without rules leads to inefficient chaos, as is often the case for start-ups.

In summary, our view of organizations is often too one-dimensional; it focuses on one attribute while neglecting others. In practice, this is not all that surprising: organizations are:

> as much closed systems as they are open systems. They are enclosed by self-fulfilling prophecies. They create the competitive environments in which they are 'forced' to compete. In doing so, they claim to be good at adaptation. In fact, they are just as good at fabrication. (Weick, 2015: 190)

Weick adds that organizing, as a practice, 'requires a balance of stability and flexibility' (Weick, 2015: 190). While organizations may appear to thrive on making rules and systems, they also need to make space for emergence and serendipity (Cunha and Berti, 2023). An excess of obtrusive rules may constitute an opportunity for rule breaking as a deliberate act of defiance (see Figure 2.2).[8]

Organizations must prepare to deal with the unexpected, despite knowing that the unexpected cannot be predicted in advance (Simpson and Clegg, 2024). Events will always happen when least expected – that is the nature of events. It is this that provides organization routines with a ritual quality, as something designed to reinforce a belief in the manageability of an uncertain world (Pierides et al., 2021).

---

[7] Available at: www.ft.com/content/10361d3f-be7c-4a6f-91c8-52a07fb9ceca

[8] Figure 2.2 was photographed by Miguel, during a conference trip in Chile. When walking in beautiful Valparaiso with my colleagues Luca Giustiniano and Arménio Rego, we found this interesting case. The litter (basura) is deposited just close to a warning: 'no botar basura' or do not litter. See how clean the rest of the setting looks.

Figure 2.2 Breaking a rule: littering next to a no littering sign in Chile (© Miguel Cunha)

The capacity to articulate different, even opposite competences, in the face of the unanticipated eventfulness of organizing, is a hedge. The case of Toyota is illustrative: the company has been described as unique in its capacity to combine a Tayloristic ethos (with its emphasis on fragmentation of work, routine and efficiency), as well as being anti-Tayloristic (with its invitation for people to think, bring change to work and revise the routines). The combination of routines and the requirement that employees rethink them incrementally reduces the ritualism of routines through continuous improvement. Routines are not ossified, reified and revered. As Japanese authors and Toyota experts Takeuchi et al. (2008) have pointed out, nobody does Taylorism as competently as Toyota yet possibly no Tayloristic organization is as anti-Tayloristic as Toyota.

Whether to explore new opportunities or exploit what is known is central to organizing (Andriopoulos and Lewis, 2009; March, 1991; Smith, 2014). Hybrid organizing introduces complexity with actors oscillating among different logics or creating novel syntheses (Jay, 2013). Where diverse and often contradictory expectations co-exist, organizations struggle to accommodate conflicting social, environmental and commercial demands, as Hahn et al. (2014) discuss. Managers face the challenge of attending to contradictory shareholder and stakeholder demands. Shareholders want profitable returns; diverse stakeholders expect returns that sustain interests in other issues, such as sustainability and community building.

Architectural practice is full of paradoxes. Powerful and wealthy client organizations want distinctive and renowned buildings to be designed to house and showcase their enterprise. They also want the buildings to be brought in on time and budget. Demands *and* making exceptional designs are not so common. Frank Gehry's buildings achieve something rare in the world of 'star architecture'. They are sensational, successful and sustainable projects. Anyone who has seen images of the Guggenheim Museum in Bilbao knows what a sensational building it is (see Figure 2.3). The sustainability is premised on waste minimization. The success of the Guggenheim Museum was in regenerating a brownfield industrial site and attracting over a million visitors a year. The sustainability is based on technology. Gehry acquired the rights to a technology initially used in Boeing aircraft design to design the sweeping curvatures, and founded Gehry Technologies to exploit the technology. While enabling more fluid, folded designs, such as the Guggenheim Museum, the technology is also essential in securing waste minimization of materials in the building process, reducing average levels of waste by over 30 per cent (Gehry et al., 2020).

Figure 2.3   The Guggenheim Museum in Bilbao, designed by Frank Gehry

Source: picture by Tony Hisgett from Birmingham, reproduced under CC BY 2.0 License.

Organizations can effectively develop differentiated roles, creating ambidextrous spaces, allowing for negotiations that enable trade-offs in design and fabrication. The trade-offs could be unlimited and apply not only in technology and architecture. For instance, an important stream of research has emerged to deal with firms acquiring some attributes of social organization, while social organizations increasingly learn from business firms. The whole area of social impact bonds, for instance, demands this reconciliation (Fraser et al., 2018).

Governance in organizations is paradoxical. In democracies, every eligible person has the right to vote in the major strategic decision as to who should govern in their name. That is the key attribute of citizenship, the democratic choice of one vote, one value, in determining who the rulers will be, with the democratic option of changing them through elections. In most organizations in most democratic countries, paradoxically, major strategic decisions are made without any reference to the employees as voters. They have little or no effective organizational citizenship. Major strategic decisions can have significant effects on employees' opportunities and their living, making the lack of any effective representations a political paradox of corporate governance. In one sphere of life, an election held periodically gives voice; in another sphere of life, employment, major strategic decisions are often implemented without any representation. While in some countries, those with co-determination systems of employee representation on strategic boards, there is some resolution of this paradox, the vast majority of countries do not have such systems in place. Instead, they have abstract representation of capital through shareholder citizenship, not on a one-vote, one-value basis, but on a basis of as many votes as shares, affording many values. With no shares and just an employment contract, no vote, no value.

In the heart of *capitalist democracies* resides this major paradox: what makes them *democratic* is universal and equal rights to decision on governance, periodically exercised; what makes them *capitalist* is the denial of such rights to those who toil for the profit accruing to the organizations that employ them. Only the board has decision rights and only shareholders can vote them in and out of governance. It is democracy for capital, with absolutism for employees, in terms of voting rights. That is the paradox of democratic capitalism.

In organizations, the job of board members, in whom governance is entrusted, is further rife with paradox. These paradoxes occur when board members, dealing with events, make choices between contradictory options and decide actions. If board members have not cultivated a majority 'paradox mindset', oppositions will not be grasped, as the board will struggle to make either/or choices. Under such circumstances, organizing can become a source of pragmatic paradoxes (see Chapter 7), generating tension created by either/or choices. The board may decide to keep on exploiting the revenue basis of existing operations – for instance, in educational publishing, thinking that the alternative option of exploring Advanced Natural Language Programming, such as GPT-4, is too exploratory, too risky. The market may decide otherwise, as Staton (2023) suggests. Individual board members supporting the excluded option can often feel disempowered or that they have lost.[9]

In the past, employees were viewed by some as experts in obedience (Jacques, 1995), but in recent times many employees have become more public and vocal about their roles in organizations. In some cases, employees have entered the public arena in terms of criticizing their organizations' defence of some external cause in an example of prosocial activism. These cross-level inconsistencies may have an important role in the identification of tension points in organizations. For instance, when an organization claims that it cares about humanity while mistreating its employees, it exposes itself to accusations of hypocrisy.

---

[9]Staton, B., 'Shares in education companies fall sharply after warning over ChatGPT', *Financial Times*, 3 May 2023, p. 3. Available at: www.ft.com/content/0db12614-324c-483c-b31c-2255e8562910

Cunha and colleagues' (2019) work on the diffusion of the value of speaking up in a pharma company demonstrates how organizations may lack tolerance of paradoxes, meaning that when paradoxical choices emerge they will be dismissed, being unrecognizable in everyday organizational language and practice. However, the relationship between board strategy and those executives that implement strategy in practice becomes more fruitful when a board that embraces paradox creates power dynamics favourable to voice – a voice that not only cascades down the organization but which flows up as well. In this case, contradictions can be rendered salient and treated as central facets of organizations, because they are being observed from different interests, interests that are empowered to speak up. Elite rights to executive decisions articulate with a multitude of perspectives and conflicting points of view, creating tensions that organizations can use as 'idea work' (Carlsen et al., 2012; Coldevin et al., 2019), serving as a source of organizational creativity and renewal.

Paradoxes may also originate because of cross-level tensions or inconsistencies. For example, as organizations are pressured to embrace corporate social responsibility (CSR) initiatives, they risk creating tensions, given that few subjects in management and organization studies generate more controversy than CSR. This happens for a number of reasons. First, when an organization makes positive claims about its social impact, it immediately attracts attention and extra scrutiny.[10] It is always interesting to identity corporate false claims and expressions of corporate 'window dressing' and 'greenwashing'. Second, different stakeholders necessarily do have different ways of understanding CSR and priorities may differ. For example, the employees of a large retail company may consider that salaries are the utmost priority for reasons of justice, whereas an environmental group may instead favour sustainability factors. Third, groups have become more vocal about their interests and, for this reason, disagreements became more public and explicit (Hahn et al., 2023).

Much research on managing paradoxes focuses on what goes on within an organization's boundaries. Not all research, though, does this. Jarzabkowski et al. (2022) explored paradoxes occurring in interorganizational systems that involve multiple actors across boundaries. They offered a process framework showing the dynamics involved in navigating multiple interorganizational paradoxes, as discussed next.

Interorganizational level paradoxes: Multiple organizations can be involved in paradoxes as a result of their interorganizational relations. When organizations engage in both competition and collaboration (Gnyawali and Park, 2011), interorganizational paradox may be evident. Pamphile's (2022) work on navigating business and societal demands shows that paradoxes are managed relationally by crossing boundaries. Organizations *collaborate* with suppliers and form associations with other organizations from the same sector to protect common interests. They also *compete* in markets with other organizations offering similar products or services. Sometimes they cooperate *and* compete in the process called *coopetition*, the simultaneous relation of cooperation and competition – for example, where competitors partner in a joint venture (Raza-Ullah

---

[10]Hill, A. 'Family firms: The succession trap', *Financial Times*, 13 March 2023, p. 15.

et al., 2014). Organizations engage in complex contradictory relationships. Knowing how to manage these is crucial to gain and sustain a competitive edge.

Akin to interorganizational paradoxes are multisectoral paradoxes, occurring as a result of collaborating organizations experimenting with fluid forms of leadership, embedded in a system rather than embodied in a person (Uhl-Bien et al., 2007). Multi-stakeholder and multisector collaborations, such as those corresponding to open innovation, provide examples. Such organizations try not only to increase their capacity to respond to changing environments, but also to change these environments to provide better answers to pressing problems affecting a plurality of stakeholders. Yet even distributed systems need some form of coordination. Therefore, even though distributed leadership does not require an apex, it requires a relational centre, a central node in its network, maintaining tension between distributing and retaining leadership, between centre and peripheries. The paradox in the process concerns how to articulate *distribution* and *centralization*, in a fruitful way, over time. These opposed forces must exist in a state of paradoxical synergy, of interpenetration, meaning that the centre *both* distributes leadership *and* retains leadership (Smith et al., 2016). A healthy tension between empowering actors for some actions but not for others provides central nodal points with a desirable equilibrium, founded upon action nets of relations.

Societal level: Societies are also crossed by paradoxical choices and tensions. For example, democracy is a system that accommodates different ideologies and worldviews in a state of differentiation and integration. These oppositions have to coexist in a fruitful way as they constitute the very core of the democratic project; the proliferation of calculated lies in the public sphere, spread by both politicians and media who know that these are lies, threaten democratic relations of differentiation and integration. The world saw this in the attempted insurrection in the US Congress on 6 January 2021, as well as in the subsequent successful lawsuit by Dominion against News Corp for spreading the falsehood that the 2020 election had been stolen through manipulation of their voting machines.

Other tensions permeate modern societies as well. In the wake of the 9/11 attacks in the US, a prominent question was how much freedom are we ready to sacrifice in the name of security? Contemporaneously, it is asked what data will we offer to companies in the surveillance economy (Zuboff, 2022)? How much difference do we welcome before considering that collective identity is endangered? All these are crucial questions for contemporary societies. They all contain an element of tension and contradiction. Consider the macro-challenges confronting decision-makers in the European Union:

> There is a contradiction [...] between the goals of more investment, strictly constraints on national budgets and no additional common spending. The future of Europe's economy depends on resolving this trilemma.[11]

---

[11]Sandbu, M., *Financial Times*, 2 July 2023, p. 23. Available at: www.ft.com/content/8a6a8bb8-7d98-4a9c-9d4f-afcef6805f3a

Final note

In this chapter, we introduced you to the fundamentals of competing demands and how they are problematized and visualized. Problematizing and visualizing are not just intellectual exercises because they have practical implications, framing what is seen and what is not seen as relevant. The way we see or do not recognize phenomena, as well as the language and metaphors we use to represent what we see, inform our decisions and responses. In this chapter, we underscored the importance of how problematizing and visualizing competing demands set the stage for how they are understood and managed. Most importantly, we distinguished paradox from adjacent concepts such as dilemmas and trade-offs. Foundations for understanding the different levels at which paradoxes occur have been prepared. In future, choosing either one or the other binary courses of action may be thought of differently; instead, there may be paradoxes to explore.

3

Types of Paradoxes

This chapter presents paradoxes and the different ways they become manifest in organizations. We discuss the central works of Wendy Smith and Marianne Lewis, and consider the four typologies of paradox they have developed. The four paradoxes focus on the questions of what (performing paradox), when (the learning paradox), who (the belonging paradox) and how (organizing paradox). Granted, these paradoxes do not operate independently; rather, they are interdependent and influence each other. The interdependent nature of the paradoxes is presented towards the end of the chapter.

Based on the foundational work of Wendy Smith and Marianne Lewis, we now explain four major types of paradoxes. These paradoxes are linked to core activities of organizations (*knowledge, identity, processes, goals*) and to crucial questions for those creating and running organizations, such as '*what* they are going to do, *how* they are going to do it, *who* is going to do it, and in *what time horizon*' (Smith and Lewis, 2011: 388). First, as leaders decide *what* to do and what not to do, the focus becomes one of what goals to achieve. *Performing paradoxes,* such as striving for both social and commercial goals, can arise. Second, as leaders define *how* they will operate, the decision creates *organizing paradoxes*, such as using greater or lesser centralization or decentralization. Third, as decisions are made as to *who* will do what, conflicting identities (roles and values) can be triggered, creating *belonging paradoxes*. Fourth, as the time horizon for actions is considered, decision-makers face a *learning paradox* – for example, between doing something immediately or in the future (Smith and Lewis, 2011).

Paradoxes of learning

Established firms tend to focus on what has worked in the past, neglecting the future in what is sometimes referred to as the Icarus paradox (also see Box 2.1). The paradox of success resides in the fact that the very thing that makes success could also be the reason for failure. Think of Kodak which failed to adjust from processing celluloid negatives from the film used in cameras to the replacement of these cameras by digital devices, such as smart phones. Kodak was a firm that understood chemical processes extremely well. The trouble was that old-style cameras, relying on the chemical processing of negatives, were in steep decline as digital cameras, especially in smart phones, outflanked print-based photography. Cameras using film mostly disappeared, except for specialist photographers (Munir and Phillips, 2005). With the decline of old-style cameras, the market for rolls of film and the processing of their negatives dried up. Kodak stuck to what it was good at. As it stayed loyal to its tradition, the market changed and it failed to change with it.

Organization leaders have to deal with the needs of today *and* tomorrow, focusing on building upon the past to create the future, looking forwards and looking backwards simultaneously (Andriopoulos and Lewis, 2010). Sometimes the past has to be superseded rather than becoming something in which one is stuck. Organization leaders must engage in adjusting *and* innovating, usually referred to as the challenge of *exploring and exploiting* after influential work by the late James March (1991).

Organizations must learn, but organizational learning constitutes an oxymoron (Weick and Westley, 1999). To organize is to establish routines, standard procedures, formal relations of authority, etc. Learning is not just about adding to existing knowledge; more vitally, it is about disrupting it, achieving breakthroughs, innovations, changing direction. While organizations benefit from learning, different learning routines produce distinct results – given their combinations of exploration/exploitation and internal/external orientations. Learning in teams and organizations therefore implies the consideration of important trade-offs, such as a measure of process standardization and employee empowerment (Ton, 2023). For example, a focus on internal-exploitation learning will potentially result in an excess of convergence that can, over time, put an organization out of sync with external changes (Harvey et al., 2022). Organizations have to traverse time by learning to cope with its challenges, while they must transgress what they already know to learn what they do not know (Vince, 2018; Weick and Westley, 1999). Otherwise, they create a rut or a groove, composed of routines that have worked in the past from which they cannot escape – the Kodak trap.

Established organizations usually have in-house R&D working on future projects to build on current capabilities, or to destroy and replace them with new possibilities. Organizations that wholly focus on current capabilities tend to disappear, regardless of their initial success and vast resources. Blockbuster was good at rolling out video stores, but was unable to see that the future of the industry was in digital streaming, so much so that when it was offered Netflix in 2000, it didn't want to buy it. According to Reed Hastings, founder of Netflix, Blockbuster was overoptimized for a single thing which it was very good at doing, but lacked the skills necessary to continue to thrive and survive. Nokia had about 38.6 per cent of the mobile market share in 2008, but failed to adapt from flip phones to smartphones and now stands at just under 1 per cent. Blackberry dominated the mobile phone market after seizing it from Nokia, only to lose it quite rapidly to Apple and other smart phones.

The taxi and hotel industries have been disrupted by innovative start-ups such as Uber and Airbnb. They resulted from entrepreneurial digital solutions to issues that the incumbent industry giants never considered.

Corporations such as ABB, Microsoft and Ericsson have established corporate accelerators to attract start-ups and work on various project to renew themselves. On top of in-house R&D and corporate accelerators, established firms collaborate with start-ups to access new technologies and teams that could potentially replace them or change them in a significant way. Corporates also join intermediaries, such as Ignite Sweden, which create a space for them and for start-ups to establish new ties and co-create (Gaim et al., 2020; Nair and Gaim, 2023).

Working with start-ups helps corporates to manage the paradox of learning, as they can fund new solutions, technologies and business models using vast existing resources and capabilities. Their collaboration is a win–win as:

> corporations and start-ups can both yield tremendous value when they collaborate with one another. Start-ups can offer corporations novel ideas and process flexibility, while corporations can provide significant resources and process efficiency. (Gaim et al., 2022: 1)

Such collaborations enable organizational innovation, 'building upon, as well as destroying, the past to create the future' (Smith and Lewis, 2011: 383). In addition, the paradox of learning also includes the decision of whether to change incrementally or radically. Each choice requires a unique strategy and structure (Ettlie et al., 1984).

Paradoxes of organizing

Paradoxes of organizing entail leaders being challenged simultaneously to direct and empower, compete and collaborate, to focus on both control and flexibility (Smith and Lewis, 2011: 383). Fundamental design decisions (Cunha et al., 2022) must be made about issues such as empowerment and direction (Denison et al., 1995), efficiency and flexibility (Adler et al., 1999), competition and collaboration (Raza-Ullah et al., 2014). Organizing can be 'loosely coupled versus tightly coupled, centralized versus decentralized, and flexible versus controlling' (Smith and Lewis, 2011: 388). Other notable areas for decision making include how to tackle differentiation and integration (Lawrence and Lorsch, 1967) and planning and improvising (Cunha et al., 2024). For instance, while it is important to use formalized planning tools (Puyt et al., 2023), it is also important to be mindful of the limitations of plans (Mintzberg, 1984). Plans can lock you into futures that, because of events, rapidly become different from those planned. But emerging 'agile' forms, such as holacracies (Schell and Bischof, 2022), also bring their challenges, including the emergence of informal hierarchies in non-hierarchical organizations.

If we consider projects, the paradoxes of organizing become even more evident. Projects, despite being temporary organizations, tend to endure through the traces they leave long after their completion (Clegg et al., 2020). Moreover, as temporary organizations, projects exhibit a tension between how they are 'decoupled from' vs 'embedded in' permanent organizations, between functioning autonomously or depending on the permanent organization for resources (Burke and Morley, 2016). Projects are crucial for societies meeting grand challenges, such as building a broadband network, transforming to renewable energy, or building a next-generation defence capability, such as nuclear submarines replacing diesel-powered vessels. Managing such projects confronts policymakers and project managers with a number of competing demands. These include quality and costs, as well as different temporal horizons to bring the project in on time but without sacrificing long-term quality or blowing the budget.

Project management has been described as a paradoxical profession (Sabini and Alderman, 2021). Really large projects, known as megaprojects, comprise complex ventures elaborated over time, with huge budgets. To the extent that their planning has no prior projects to which they can easily refer for precedents, such projects will invariably be fraught with significant planning difficulties. Professionals have to design unique projects whose planning they can reasonably expect will fail.

Flyvbjerg and Gardner (2023) suggest that projects fail because of human biases, such as the optimism bias, a tendency to overestimate the chances that the project will go well, and the cost–benefit fallacy, a situation where individuals assume that cost–benefit estimates are to a great extent accurate, while in practice these are often inaccurate and biased. In addition, it is suggested that planners often deliberately distort or misstate information to serve their interests – personal or professional (Lovallo et al., 2023).

The nature of project success and failure has become a scholarly battlefield. As Kreiner (2020) argues, projects always entail risks, as the uncertainties and difficulties that will unfold in the future cause people to take more significant risks than they intend. To attribute an initial bias or distortion to project failures in terms of cost, schedule and benefits is to propose that professionals routinely behave in ways that are unprofessional. We know that sometimes they might; we do not know that nearly always they will. What is being proposed is done on the basis of little evidence other than a post-hoc rationalization that if initial plans are not realized, then individuals' cognitive processes must be responsible. There is frequently little evidence connecting these presumed biases and the project processes that ensue. Project processes create futures that are invariably unpredictable in all their features; organizations plan in order to minimize these, but in the face of unique and complex projects unfolding over time and encountering unknown variables, it is hardly surprising if plans have to be updated, improvisations made, costs accrued and futures altered.

The world of major projects is paradoxical in that project failure in terms of cost, schedule and benefits happens repeatedly, not because of a conspiracy of bias making for bad planning, but because such projects have innate risks that even the best planning and project management cannot predict. In open systems, with infinite variables, prediction is a chimera and paradox an ever-present possibility. What is important is how paradox is used: is it as something to be suppressed in the light of plans made in partial ignorance of the events defining the present situation, or as an opportunity for creativity, ingenuity and paradoxical idea work?

Beyond projects, multiple models with the objective of making organizations more flexible and flatter, comprising self-organizing teams, have proliferated (Lee and Edmondson, 2017). These models intensify the paradox of organizing, especially in balancing flexibility and control. Notable organizations have flattened their structure and relinquished hierarchies, such as Zappos, Oticon and Valve. For example, in the case of Oticon, the highly distributed 'spaghetti organization' it instituted, ran its course until the organization, facing too much complexity, introduced some control over its work by switching to a more stable matrix structure (Gaim and Wåhlin, 2016). Others, such as Valve, instituted a control mechanism not based on the usual hierarchy or direct control. Felin (2014) singled out the rule of three among the design features that Valve introduced. The rule of three:

> [R]equires that at least three individuals within the organization agree that a particular initiative, product idea, or project is worth pursuing before it is launched. Not only should three individuals agree about the value of the project, but they also need to be willing to join and work on the project. Thus, unlike polyarchies (in their pure form), Valve has instituted a practice where individuals cannot pursue projects on their own. Every initiative and project require a threshold level of social support – in effect, creating a tipping point (of three individuals) for action. (Felin, 2014: 10)

Regardless of debureaucratization attempts, the necessity of bureaucracy and bosses is still regarded as dominant (Foss and Klein, 2022). As Cunha et al. (2022: 112) note:

> while even non-hierarchical organizations do not free themselves from hierarchy, they limit it to the minimum necessary to keep the organization coordinated without unnecessary control or control for control's sake. It is safe to say that hierarchy has not perished but rather it is fading and being replaced by other forms of organizing to structure fluid work and unstructured workers.

Netflix is known for its 'no rule rules' (Hastings and Meyer, 2020) where traditional hierarchy is absent. As illustrated in Hastings and Meyer (2020), Netflix operates without the traditional hierarchy and rule structure. The focus is on hiring the best people, empowering them and trusting their judgement. Instead of hierarchy, Hastings described Netflix as a tree. Hastings explained Netflix in the following terms:

> In a tree, the trunk is supporting all the branches which do all the work, the leaves, the photosynthesis, the nutrients. And so, we look at our leadership team as the trunk supporting all of the real work, rather than being at the top of an organization, sort of like the king.[1]

---

[1]Available at: https://freakonomics.com/podcast/what-if-your-company-had-no-rules-bonus-episode/. The metaphor is clear but not entirely apt; it is the rhizomatic structure beneath the ground that does the real work of sustaining the tree. To extend the metaphor, the rhizomatic structure is the networks of employees and suppliers sustaining the leadership.

Hierarchy is thus replaced by talent density, hiring the best people. A system that empowers employees to make the right decision, instead of telling them what to do and what not to do, has been installed. This might seem quite paradoxical to traditional views of efficiency being a matter of tight control; here, by contrast, efficiency is seen to be served by a paradoxically diminishing hierarchy.

Modelling behaviour on leaders practising what they preach (for example, Hastings is known to take lot of vacation days), allows employees to develop a social understanding and culture. In Netflix, this centres on issues such as how many hours to work a day on average (work hours are not regulated) and leading by context (instead of direct control). Hastings explained leading by context as follows:

> Control is when you tell someone specifically to do something. 'Let's cancel that advertisement. That makes us look bad.' And then, context would be 'we're generally trying to connect with consumers. What is making us do this advertisement?' And really trying to understand what the motivation is. And then, if the person says, 'Well, you keep talking how we want to be must-see T.V., kind of essential viewing, and so that's how I came up with this addiction advertisement.' And then you can say, 'Okay, I can see that the context that I set, which is we want to be seen as essential, wasn't specific enough. And instead, we want to be seen as a part of everyday life but not generating addictive behaviours.' And that I needed to improve the context. And thus, by improving the context, it would probably have good application in many other parts of the business in addition to, say, this group doing the advertising.[2]

As March and Weil (2009: 98) noted: 'if power is not used as an instrument for winning personal influence, but as a means of encouraging other people to blossom, its charms can be enjoyed while the fear that it inspires is minimized'. It has been suggested further that:

> Leaders who know when and how to cede power earn respect and commitment. The best people want to work for them, and the team member with the most pertinent expertise sways decisions. For all those reasons, their teams perform better. (Greer et al., 2023: 80)

Similarly, we expect leaders to embrace paradoxes enabling them to be cunning and authentic, firm and soft, ruthless and compassionate, all at the same time. New Zealand ex-Prime Minister Jacinda Ardern, reflecting on her leadership style, said:

> One of the criticisms I've faced over the years is that I'm not aggressive enough or assertive enough, or maybe somehow, because I'm empathetic, it means I'm weak. I totally rebel against that. I refuse to believe that you cannot be both compassionate and strong.[3]

---

[2] Available at: https://freakonomics.com/podcast/what-if-your-company-had-no-rules-bonus-episode/
[3] Dowd, M., 'Lady of the Rings: Jacinda Rules', *The New York Times*, 8 September 2018. Available at: www.nytimes.com/2018/09/08/opinion/sunday/jacinda-ardern-new-zealand-prime-minister.html

It might be the case that while we may need humble, emotionally mature leaders enough voters still become infatuated with grand narcissists such as Trump, Johnson and Netanhayu – note they're all male. Maybe we should look for those that are 'humbitious' (i.e., humble and ambitious), praised for being bold *and* for being unimposing (Tan, 2023). Working in cultures that are strong does not mean that they have to be totalitarian. The organizations we work in need solid routines as well as innovation pipelines, creativity as well as predictability. Organizations exist in markets that are engines of creative destruction; neither ritual rule-following nor a thousand flowers blooming are guarantees against these risks.

In summary, the world of organizations is criss-crossed by competing demands. It is because of the growing awareness of this facet that the ability to articulate paradoxes is viewed by some scholars as *the* critical new competence for managers (Lewis and Smith, 2023): 'if you are leading an organization – large or small – you may be feeling mounting pressure to navigate paradoxes' (Lewis and Smith, 2023: 12).

Box 3.1   Autonomy vs compliance

Organizations often expose their members to a paradox between autonomy and compliance. Public organizations often make this more difficult to navigate because results are often defined by distant supra-organizational decision-makers, leading to absurd situations.

For example, one of the authors of this book has been asked in his school over the years to include the fiscal number of the school in the receipt of conference registrations. The fact that some conference websites do not have a space for this information does not prevent the services from repeating the request.

But there are other rules for accommodation: public servants cannot stay in hotels above 3 stars and above a certain pre-established price. It happened once that the options included 4-star hotels below the price range and 3-star hotels above. Faced with the choice, our academic was asked where he wanted to stay. The obvious choice, the 4-star hotel was *not possible within the rules*. The second choice was also *impossible because it breached the rules*. In the end, he stayed in a 2-star B&B, in a good illustration of how people are sometimes 'neutralized' by dumb rules.

As the illustration in Box 3.1 suggests, the paradox between autonomy and compliance can often lead to absurd and bizarre situations. In *Life and Fate*, Vassily Grossman's masterpiece (Grossman, 2011), there is an illustrative story of a Soviet military unit surrounded by Nazis, meaning that they could only be supplied from the air. But food and other goods could only be supplied in exchange for a signed document: no document, no supplies. It took some time for the absurd requirement to be corrected. Thus, while rules and compliance do matter, there must be an ele-ment of dialogue to manage the paradox between compliance and autonomy in order to manage the rules 'on the ground' (Ragaigne, 2023). In the absence of dia-logue, paradoxes may become paralysing.

The classical statement of this paradoxical absurdity is Joseph Heller's *Catch-22*. In the novel, Captain John Yossarian is an American bombardier stuck on a Mediterranean island during the Second World War. Yossarian is determined to stay alive by not flying missions, which is thwarted by 'catch-22'. This regulation stipulates that a pilot may request to be grounded if he pleads insanity, but that if he is sane enough to know that flying missions is insane, he is deemed to be of sound mind. Catch-22 was perfect because it could not be negotiated; there was no dialogue that could get around it.

Paradoxes of performing

Paradoxes of performing result from attempting to accommodate multiple internal and external stakeholders, as well as from addressing the internal challenges of get-ting work done. Individuals feel tensions between the internal goods of the practice, the values associated with it (such as care in the case of medical doctors), and the external values it brings such as fame and money, as well as the contingencies faced (Hadjimichael and Tsoukas, 2023). Additionally, as workers we have to navigate tensions: between institutional constraints and individual autonomy, such as in the case of knowledge workers, professionals and academics (Petriglieri and Ashford, 2023), and between independence and precarity, in the case of independent workers in the gig economy (Petriglieri et al., 2019).

At the level of organization, having to accommodate social, economic and envi-ronmental demands typifies the paradox of performing (Hahn et al., 2014). As leaders decide on what they wanted to do, they also decide on what not to do. As they define their goals and strategies, they can trigger a performing paradox, such as being 'global versus local and socially focused versus financially focused' (Smith and Lewis, 2011: 388).

Consider the case of social media platforms, such as Facebook and Twitter (now rebranded as 'X'). Their challenge is content moderation. What makes money (hence is profitable for the company) is not necessarily good for the audience (social media users and the general society). In addition, given the polarized political space, what is right for one stakeholder might not be right for others. For example, banning Donald Trump from social media platforms was the epitome of the discussion about content moderation that tested the delicate line between hate speech and the love of freedom of speech.

The importance of providing timely and accurate information about COVID-19 has also been a polarizing topic. As different actors using social media had differ-ent values, priorities and preferences about the spread of COVID-19, it meant that social media platforms had to decide what to censor and what not to censor, given the millions of user-generated contents. Some things being promulgated, even by the then President of the United States, were not only ridiculously unscientific but also downright dangerous. A glass of bleach, anyone? Twitter was leading the content moderation space until Elon Musk's takeover. On top of resources being limited after laying off almost half of the company's 7,500 employees, his absolutist stance allowing any free speech changed the trajectory of content moderation.

Sustainability is another sphere in which paradox abounds. Metal straws are increasingly used to limit disposal of unsustainable plastic straws that end up in landfill and waterways. A 'sustainability paradox' accompanies the switch, however. Metal straws need washing in hot water to make them useable by another person. However, as Mark Falinski[4] notes, a single metal straw would need to be used over 100 times to negate the emissions impacts of making and washing it. A 20-pack of straws would have to be used nearly 2,500 times to negate the equivalent emissions in terms of the carbon life cycle. What appears more sustainable is, in fact, far less so. Paradoxically, it is not easy being green.

Box 3.2   Trains and planes

Some approaches that managers take towards sustainability are unusual. For example, in 2022, Marjan Rintel, the CEO of KLM, the Dutch commercial airline, invited travellers and potential customers to take the train, when possible, for environmental reasons. 'If [you] have a good alternative, you should really use it,' Marjan Rintel told the *Financial Times* in an interview. 'If you're serious on reaching your sustainability goals, the train is not a competitor. We need to work together.' The point is obvious. But is it? Consider the CEO's suggestion from the following perspectives: as a board member, an employee, a competitor, a customer/traveller, an environmental activist, a consultant. If no other airline makes equivalent recommendations, what would you recommend to the board? Is there a paradox in the invitation? Why?

Similarly, think, for example, of the decision to manufacture or purchase an e-vehicle on sustainability grounds. For how many years does the vehicle have to be on the road and how many miles must it drive to be more sustainable than an existing petrol-engine vehicle? How sustainable are the manufacturing processes creating the vehicle? What is the energy derived from manufacturing the vehicle? In a rapidly changing world, these are paradoxes that many of us that are fortunate enough to be able to aspire to personal means of mobility must face. These paradoxes also confront the organizations that manufacture mobility devices. We have mentioned an earlier paradoxical relation between managing emissions and impression management when one manufacturer, VW, failed to handle the paradox successfully (Gaim et al., 2021). As diesel

---

[4]Available at: https://choosefinch.com/blog/the-sustainability-paradox-the-pros-and-cons-of-doing-good#:~:text=This%20is%20what%20we%20call,causing%20new%2C%20unintended%20damage%20elsewhere

becomes history and as transitions to e-vehicles become increasingly common, there will be many competing demands for both manufacturers and users.

There are many other paradoxes of sustainability that you can investigate (Hahn et al., 2018) that capture the performing paradox. Consider the increasing pressure for managers to attend to the triple bottom line. Instead of focusing on one goal – traditionally, profit (Friedman, 1970), managers are now pressured to integrate benefits for people, planet and profits. Of course, the three exist in a state of tension, as more attention (and resources) to one may correspond to less being available for the others.

Navigating paradox is an exercise in finding synergies between oppositions. Doing so can be problematic and debilitating, as oppositions divide sides and create divergent views, focusing on one pole at the cost of the other. Working with paradox can be difficult, as complex themes require complex approaches. The challenges involved in the pursuit of sustainability goals at the expense of economic goals can be seen in the demise of the former CEO of Danone, Emmanuel Faber. As the press reported, 'Faber had turned Danone into an *"enterprise à mission"*', France's new category similar to an American B-Corp, whose purpose was far broader than profits and growth. He named his strategy 'One Planet, One Health', and created a carbon-adjusted earnings per share indicator, pegging Danone's success directly to its environmental performance. While that brought applause from climate activists, during the pandemic the company's shares lagged behind peers like Nestlé and Unilever, as sales of some key Danone products, such as Evian water, plummeted (also see Box 3.2 for Marjan Rintel's unusual approach to sustainability).[5]

Similarly, geopolitics also dictate how leaders in politics, global institutions such as the UN, as well as business organizations, handle the paradox of morality and commercial/political interest:

> CEOs who play moralists with respect to Vladimir Putin are hard-pressed to justify – in ethical terms, if not financial ones – why they embrace realpolitik when it comes to Xi Jinping. Mr. Putin's war crimes are atrocious, but are they different in kind from the mistreatment of Uyghurs, which the Biden administration has called 'genocide'?[6]

Managers should view paradoxes as an inevitable feature of the reality of organizations (Lewis et al., 2014), embracing them rather than trying to eliminate them.

Paradoxes of belonging

The paradoxes of belonging arise as organizational actors navigate their place as individuals and as part of a group, maintaining their distinctiveness, while subject

---

[5]Available at: https://time.com/6121684/emmanuel-faber-danone-interview/

[6]'The reluctant rise of the diplomat CEO', *The Economist*, 27 October 2022, p. 66. Available at: www.economist.com/business/2022/10/27/the-reluctant-rise-of-the-diplomat-ceo

to pressures for homogeneity (Smith and Berg, 1987). A paradox of belonging raises questions of identity. As organizational actors assume different roles, memberships and values, they may try to adopt competing interests (Smith and Lewis, 2011). For example, architects who value aesthetics might face a challenge when assuming managerial positions (Gaim, 2018) as they navigate the paradox of what they are to value. Similarly, artists may focus on art but are forced to accommodate commercial demands, realizing that art for art's sake is not economically sustainable as it involves waiting for the market to reward one's passions (Eikhof and Haunschild, 2007).

Waiting for recognition and managing in the meantime can create significant emotional pain, as happened with the founder of music label 4AD, which we mentioned earlier. Ivo Watts Russell, the founder, created a company to produce great music, for the love of music. The label was successful and he found himself at the helm of what became an increasingly commercial operation. Tensions developed between pressures for commercial success that were incompatible with his commitment to the music (see Cunha et al., 2019). Other artists, such as famous street artist Banksy, manage to keep a vibrant space within the art market while simultaneously being an anonymous outsider (Cunha et al., 2021).

Most cultural institutions, according to Glynn (2000: 285), encompass identities that are contradictory 'because they contain actors (artisans and administrators) within the organization who come from different professions; as a result, different groups of actors cherish and promote different aspects of the organization's identity'. Using the case of the Atlanta Symphony Orchestra, Glynn (2000) explains the tensions between artistic values and commercial imperatives at work. The two professional tropes (i.e., musicians and administrators) have different prescriptions for action when it comes to the orchestra's allocation of resources. As she states:

> [C]onsistent with the legitimating values of their profession, the musicians emphasized investment in artistry, and administrators, seeking a demonstration of fiscal responsibility, emphasized cost containment. Each group felt that their prestige, legitimization, and power to influence others rested on their ability to realize such outcomes. (Glynn, 2000: 295)

Some members of the orchestra were passionately committed to ideals of classical music, while other members wished to make classical music more popular and more accessible to the public (Lampel et al., 2000). In such settings:

> tensions cannot be easily resolved. At best, a balance is struck. When the balance is toppled by crisis, each side champions its own values, inevitably producing an open conflict between art and entertainment. Ultimately neither can prevail without destroying the identity of the organization as a symphonic orchestra; coexistence is the only option. (Lampel et al., 2000: 266)

Given that we all have multiple identities and that we usually cannot switch off one while assuming the other, we live with the paradox of belonging in our day-to-day life. For example, as a working parent, when thinking about how much time and energy to allocate to work and life, we are navigating the belonging paradox of being both a good parent and a good employee (Smith and Lewis, 2022).

The interrelatedness of paradoxes

In practice, paradoxes are interrelated. According to Smith and Lewis (2011), tensions operate interstitially as well as categorically. For example, as was shown in Glynn's (2000) work, performing and belonging paradoxes are at play at the same time, the opposition between goals and priorities (i.e., art vs commerce) triggering the belonging paradox as actors negotiate their identity (Smith and Lewis, 2011). In their study of an NGO, Lempiälä et al. (2022) show how managing idealistic and pragmatic goals in daily practices gives rise to interconnected paradoxes of performing and belonging where the conflicting objectives trigger identity conflict at individual and group levels. In their study, the authors show how:

> [P]erforming paradoxes triggered belonging paradoxes as the fact that the group members flexibly argued for either polarity of the performing paradox conflicted with the expectation of the group being uniformly positioned on the side of idealistic values. Interestingly, the group then constructed the organization-level performing paradox between funders' requirements and the organization's social mission in order to reframe the group-internal value tensions to exist between the organization and external actors. (Lempiälä et al., 2022: 2)

In another study in a hospital emergency room, interrelated paradoxes of learning and organizing were evident. Organizational actors sought to maintain stability (compliance) of routines while remaining flexible to accommodate emergencies; at the same time (see Box 3.3), they focused on being efficient (releasing patients in a given time frame), while allowing enough time for juniors to learn in the process (Rosales et al., 2022).

Box 3.3 Is change stable? Is stability change?

The image of the ouroboros is well known: a serpent eating its own tail. The earliest record of this image (thirteenth-century BCE) was found on a golden shrine in the tomb of Tutankhamen, the Egyptian king. It was used to depict the Egyptian understanding of time. To ancient Egyptians, time was not linear, an arrow, but instead a continuous series of repetitive cycles, mirroring the flooding of the Nile or the journey of the sun (see Kets de Vries, 2023).

Figure 3.1   The ouroboros

Source: Openclipart.org

Based on this image, how would you think about time and change? Does time unfold mere repetition? Can repetition be change?

We return once more to Elon Musk. Musk is dealing with multiple and interrelated paradoxes. He was already CEO of multiple multi-billion dollar companies when he purchased Twitter (now rebranded as 'X'). The acquisition has been controversial in several ways, especially in terms of how his attention is now spread over several unrelated product-based portfolios. Tesla investors have called for him to focus. According to a report in *The Washington Post*, 'Now, some Tesla investors are calling for Musk to hand over the reins at one of his companies as the electric vehicle company's stock plummets – raising concerns that the billionaire is stretched too thin.'[7]

For a leader, dealing with interrelated paradoxes means drawing from two essential elements of leadership: plumbing and poetry (March and Weil, 2009). Plumbing is 'the capacity to apply known techniques effectively', while poetry 'draws on a leader's great actions and identity and pushes him or her to explore unexpected avenues, discover interesting meanings and approach life with enthusiasm' (March and Weil, 2009: 98). The plumbing of leadership is making sure that the 'toilets work and there is somebody to answer the telephone' (2009: 98); the gift of a poet focuses on rendering life attractive and 'the formation and dissemination of interesting interpretations of reality' (2009: 98), forming a basis for constructive collective action.

---

[7]Available at: www.washingtonpost.com/technology/2022/12/15/elon-musk-tesla-twitter/

While poets' visions gain glory, boring plumbers constitute the epitome of good management. In the footsteps of March and Weil (2009) we defend the importance of poetry in leaders. Organizations need the right kind of poetry. Some leaders appear poetic because of their narcissistic traits. They appear to be attractive, self-confident, even grandiose, which is a dangerous form of poetry. Organizations should build lines of defence against these leaders (Cunha et al., 2024). Organizations need poets dedicated to the collective and to those it employs and serves. These people are the solid architects of good organizing. They provide positive role models of conscientiousness, reliability and dedication to customers. In other words, we should search for poetry in normal, even boring managers (Chamorro-Premuzic, 2022). Instead of searching for narcissistic charismatics, we need *adequate* managers (Hay, 2022).

In a recent article, Greer et al. (2023) suggested that good leaders use two 'leadership gears'. They noted that it is a 'false choice' between choosing to lead either from the front or getting out of the way. Successful leaders routinely shift between taking charge and empowering their followers in a bimodal leadership approach (a combination of the '*exercise authority* mode' and the '*flat* mode'). When leaders get stuck in one mode, they run into trouble, including not generating innovative and creative thinking (when stuck in authority mode) or lacking crisp decision-making and disciplined coordination (in the flat mode). In fact, paradox can be viewed as a form of articulation of competing demands at several levels of the organization. These cases illustrate the duality of leadership and indicate why leadership is difficult: leaders have to do one thing *and* its very opposite.

Final note

In this chapter, we presented four types of paradoxes faced by organizational actors, including leaders, based on the work of Smith and Lewis (2011). The paradoxes of *learning* refer to the challenge of managing the needs of both today and tomorrow, requiring leaders to build upon and destroy the past to create the future. The paradoxes of *organizing* involve leaders being challenged to direct and empower, compete and collaborate, and focus both on control and flexibility. We also discuss the paradoxes of *performing*, which arise from the need to balance different internal and external stakeholders, such as social, economic and environmental demands. The pressure for managers to attend to the triple bottom line presents a challenge to find synergies between oppositions. Leaders who prioritize sustainability goals over economic goals may face challenges, and the pursuit of sustainability goals can lead to their demise. Paradoxes of *belonging* centre on identity in which diverse organizational actors assume opposing roles, memberships and values.

4

Philosophical Roots and Basic Assumptions of Paradoxes

This chapter delves into the philosophical traditions that inform our under-standing of paradoxes and how we deal with them. We will, in an accessible way, explore traditions from the East, West and beyond. The development of paradox theory has its roots in various philosophical traditions. The basic assumptions used in theory are tied to different traditions. In this chapter, we will cover two traditions that have dominated theorizing – on one hand, there is the view that paradoxes are inherent, while on the other hand, is the view that paradoxes are represented as socially constructed. Viewed as inherent, paradoxes exist regardless of people's awareness. As socially constructed, they are a way of seeing reality or, as paradox theorists call it, creating a 'common mindset'.

East, West and beyond

Two dominant philosophical traditions (one from the 'East' and the other from the 'West') tend to inform normative and prescriptive lenses for studying paradoxes and mobilizing its power for managerial purposes (Smith et al., 2017a). The 'East' and the 'West', conceived as abstractions, have historically constituted different ways of managing complexity and uncertainty. Traditions and cultural differences have broader implications for cognition, emotion and behaviour (Spencer-Rodgers et al., 2010), reflected in the way that people feel, think and act. Different cultures promote thinking that is either more linear or non-linear, with each mode reacting differently to change (Ji et al., 2001; Peng and Nisbett, 1999).

In the West, the tendency is to view paradox as an abnormality that should be avoided (Prashantham and Eranova, 2020; Schad, 2017). Such a tradition suggests that, when making a choice, one should reject the least plausible proposition in favour of the most plausible one (Spencer-Rodgers et al., 2010).

> [The] West has tried to reduce and substitute complexity and uncertainty with simplicity and certainty, which has resulted in the dramatic advances in modern sciences in the West, while the East has attempted to embrace complexity and uncertainty with its own philosophical traditions. (Li, 2016: 49)

This means that irregularity, more than regularity, attracts most attention (Ji et al., 2001).

According to Peng and Nisbett (1999: 742):

> contradictory propositions are unacceptable by the laws of formal logic, which have been part of the Western tradition since Aristotle, and Westerners respond to propositions that have the appearance of contradiction by differentiation – deciding which of two propositions is correct.

Western tradition, including formal logic and logical positivism, plays a role in the way that organizational paradoxes are conceptualized. Paradoxes present problems: problems exist to be solved; solution entails choices. Thus, in the Western tradition, a 'rational foundation is still the law of noncontradiction, so that a satisfactory solution to contradiction is a noncontradictory one' (Peng and Nisbett, 1999: 742). According to Ji et al. (2001: 451), 'Western linear thinking may be linked to the belief that each cause has an effect and each effect is tied to a cause, and therefore each event can be described as an effect of a preceding event or a cause for a consequent event.'

Western logic is by now a near-universal code that, nonetheless, runs up against other modes of interpretation. In Eastern philosophical traditions (Buddhism, Confucianism and Taoism), paradox is the norm rather than an exception (Schad, 2017: 30) and Eastern-inspired cultures tend to embed an accommodation of contradictions (Keller et al., 2017). For example, in the Chinese Confucian tradition, reality is a process, full of contradictions, where nothing is isolated and independent but connected (Peng and Nisbett, 1999). Similarly, in other East Asian societies, Buddhist and Taoist traditions do not see contradictions as anomalies. Thinking about paradoxes tends towards both/and thinking, in which paradoxes are conceived not so much as problems but as opportunities for creativity and innovation. The yin–yang representation, frequently adopted in organizational paradox studies, is a visual token of this way of thinking (see Chapter 2). Accordingly, 'the yin and yang are dependent on each other' and such tradition 'emphasizes not only the coexistence and interpenetration of the two parts of a contradiction, but their change and transformation into one another as well' (Ji et al., 2001: 450).

Comparative studies consistently show how people from different traditions differ in the way they perceive and act when faced with contradictions (see Ji et al., 2001; Spencer-Rodgers et al., 2010). In their seminal work, Peng and Nisbett (1999: 741) concluded that:

> Chinese ways of dealing with seeming contradictions result in a dialectical or compromising approach – retaining basic elements of opposing perspectives by seeking a 'middle way.' On the other hand, European–American ways, deriving from a lay version of Aristotelian logic, result in a differentiation model that polarizes contradictory perspectives in an effort to determine which fact or position is correct.

With only a few exceptions (see, for example, Gaim and Clegg, 2021), the Afrocentric view in relation to paradoxes has not been explicitly theorized. Our recent contribution based on Ubuntu focuses on an indigenous African way of sensemaking as a tradition that accounts for differences in history, institutions, cultures and habits that can help to illuminate the relationships between paradoxes and the contexts in which they unfold (Cunha et al., 2020: 2).

The essence of Ubuntu, as well as of other indigenous worldviews (Bastien et al., 2023), refers to the idea of reciprocal relationships. It is captured in the popular sayings *Umuntu Ngumuntu Ngabantu* (Xhosa, Zulu) or *Motho ke motho ka batho ba bang* (Sotho), which are roughly translated as 'I am because you are, and you are because we are'. These phrases have two important and relevant implications for the way paradoxes are problematized and dealt with. First, there is a focus on the collective whole rather than the distinction of parts; second, there is an element of both competition and collaboration to create a common good (Gaim and Clegg, 2021: 21).

There are many communalities across traditions. Ubuntu, as one Afrocentric tradition, offers relevant wisdom and tools to understand and manage paradoxes. In our comparison of Afrocentric views with those of the East and West, we identified unique attributes based on Ubuntu (see Table 4.1).

Ubuntu focuses on humanness, harmony and continuity. Contradictions and the space they create for dialogue are valued and respected. As such, the fundamental tenet when dealing with contradiction is achieving consensus, with the bigger picture in mind. One unique aspect of Ubuntu, making it relevant to managing paradox, is its focus on the other people's needs (i.e., otherness). Otherness focuses on and makes others' needs open to influence and facilitates accepting and valuing others. In the face of competing demands, when organization actors:

> [S]tart from their own needs, the chances are that their approach to sensemaking will stress resistance rather than acceptance, as they will either attempt to dominate or end up in conflict […] starting with others' needs points to a

Table 4.1 Key features and differences in approaches

	Dominant Western approaches and assumptions about paradox	The Eastern approaches and assumptions about paradox	What the Ubuntu approach adds
Focus and expected outcome	Single 'truth' based on facts and logic aiming for efficiency and performance	Compromise and achieving the middle way	Humanness, harmony and continuity
Difference and tensions	Are an anomaly	Are a norm	Are a value in dialogue
Fundamental tenet when facing tensions	Choice of one over the other. There is one best/right way *Being right*	The mean balance and integration between the two poles *Being fair*	Achieving consensus with the big picture in mind through the understanding of the need of others and building harmony. *Ending right*
Predominant approach	Either/or	Either/and	'Both/anding'
The self and the other	Major concern for self	Concern for both self and others	Otherness (major concern for others)
Understanding of the firm	Collection of individuals	Wholeness of interdependent opposites	Group-centred interest

Source: Gaim and Clegg, 2021: 40.

different kind of acceptance compared to that commonly theorized in the paradox literature. Acceptance, in our case, is *other-focused* and is based on empathy and it starts from recognition rather than denial of the needs of the other. (Gaim and Clegg, 2021: 42).

In a situation in which polarization is high, thinking about the other might mean understanding how others think and work towards a common ground rather than intensifying polarity.

The Sankofa (meaning, 'to go back and get it') is another interesting insight on paradox coming from Africa. The Sankofa is a bird represented in Ghanaian folklore and tradition. What is unique is that this bird flies forward while looking backwards, carrying a precious egg in its mouth (see Figure 4.1). Sankofa symbolizes the idea of taking the good from the past as we move forward, respecting tradition that works. Gulati (2022) associated the Sankofa with the capacity to articulate a vision for the future, with the capacity to understand and respect tradition. Gulati explored the idea in the context of the renewal of Nordic companies such as Lego and Carlsberg via their respect for tradition (see also Schultz and Hernes, 2013).

Figure 4.1 The Sankofa

Source: Reproduced under the CC BY 2.0. License

The Sankofa, as a visual device, embraces the paradox of the past and the future, today and tomorrow, the known and the unknown. Tradition and memory show how the past can constitute a resource with which to explore the future. The message is: the past can inform the future and, as we fly forward, it is wise to look back, as taught by the Sankofa bird.

Seeking insights from different philosophies and traditions helps enrich our understandings and provides a tool to deal with paradoxical issues (Schad, 2017). As in other organizational areas, such as leadership, approaches rooted in different philosophical traditions and cultures (Keller et al., 2017) inform the way that competing demands will be met – for example, with either active or defensive responses or both, and whether they are framed as paradoxical or as dilemmas. Keller et al. (2017) note that culture, as an organizational context, creates the conditions with which individuals perceive contradictions. Similarly, studies by Peng and Nisbett (1999) demonstrate the effect of culture-specific epistemology on reasoning about contradictions, confirming that 'there are two very different cognitive traditions in the East and West' (Peng and Nisbett, 1999: 750). These are wellsprings for different agential ways of being in the world.

Depending on the culture within which individuals are embedded, whether it encourages or discourages contradictions and uncertainty, for example, people will act differently in the face of competing demands. How organizational actors deal with the work–life paradox in Sweden and the US differs, depending on the culture framing their work and life. As illustrated in Box 4.1, Swedish *lagom* and 'the American dream' inform organizational actors' decisions on how to deal with the paradox of work–life balance.

Box 4.1 Lagom: the Swedish art of balancing

Lagom is a Swedish word that typically means 'not too much, not too little' or 'just right'. It is believed to originate from the Viking custom of 'passing a horn of mead around and ensuring there is just enough for everyone to get a sip'. *Lagom* is the epitome of balance, where excess is unnecessary. It is a concept that is deeply ingrained in Swedish culture and is often used to describe a balanced way of living. *Lagom* is often associated with the idea of moderation and simplicity. It is about finding the right balance in all aspects of life, whether it be work–life balance, spending and saving, or consumption of resources. It is also about being content with what you have and not constantly striving for more. The idea is to find a middle ground where everything is in proportion while nothing is in excess. Why go over the top when you know what's just right? Living a *lagom* lifestyle means finding equilibrium in all aspects of life. It's about being a considerate guest by bringing your own bed sheets when visiting friends, adding a splash of colour to a room by painting only one feature wall, and indulging in a burger but skipping the fries in the name of moderation.

Linnea Dunne's book has some wonderful details about living a *lagom* lifestyle. See Dunne, L. (2017) *Lagom: The Swedish Art of Balanced Living*. London: Octopus.

For a Swede, balance might be a way of life and every aspect of their life would support the pursuit of balance. In the US, where achieving individual aspirations is a virtue, it is unlikely that this would be the case. Alexander Skarsgård, a Swedish actor, who has won an Emmy and Golden Globe, appeared on *The Late Show* with

Stephen Colbert, and talked about *Jantelagen* (the law of Jante). When asked whether he displayed his awards, he said no because he was born and brought up in Sweden, which meant that he was raised with a code of conduct that basically means 'don't think you are special'. There is a collective repulsion about people who have 'too much' success, money, fame or sorrow. Similar to the *lagom* that informs people's lives, *Jantelagen* is also reflected in the way that individuals live and deal with issues such as paradoxes in their working lives.

From a different geography, another concept from the ancient Indian figure of thought and logic, the tetralemma, is also one that we can draw inspiration from when dealing with competing demands. In tetralemma, there are four possibilities or propositions: (1) this (either)/considering one side of a dilemma; (2) that (or)/ considering the other side; (3) both/intermediating or integrating the two sides; (4) neither/considering the distinctions that create the two sides of a problem. There is a fifth possibility that switches from one problem to another (Kleve et al., 2020). Like Ubuntu and *lagom*, tetralemma is relevant in dealing with competing demands as it promotes a broader perspective by considering the four positions and beyond, freeing organizational members from the frequently used binary perspective.

The discussion so far is important because response to paradoxes are informed by dominant traditions that follow different ways of managing complexity and uncertainty. Tied to the philosophical traditions is also how paradoxes are viewed. We now highlight how we can approach paradoxes from two different perspectives. Accordingly, paradoxes can be objective realities (the materialist perspective) that exist in organizations, or subjective interpretations (the interpretivist perspective) that emerge from social interactions.

The materialist vs interpretivist perspectives

The materialist view regards paradoxes as an inherent feature of organizations, irrespective of interpretation. As Fairhurst (2022) put it, there are indeed 'brute facts' that impose themselves regardless of our analysis of the world. These include wars, pandemics and natural disasters – phenomena that disrupt plans, interfere with supply chains, redefine priorities (Hillmer et al., 2023). These outside factors combine with social dimensions and the inevitability of power and politics. As Clegg (1994: 164) noted: 'pluralism is inherent to organization'. Regardless of organizational actors' recognition of paradox, their existence does not depend on perception (Cameron and Quinn, 1988). Paradoxes exist in a state of latency prior to and independently of their recognition (Hahn and Knight, 2021). They are objectively real, even if not apprehended as such.

Alternatively, there is the interpretivist perspective, in which paradoxes are seen as a product of human practice and communication (Putnam et al., 2016), whereby it is actors' discursive practice that constructs paradoxes communicatively. In this camp, a paradox is revealed and made manageable, depending on how it is interpretatively constructed (Jarzabkowski and Lê, 2017; Tuckermann, 2018). When paradox is understood through the lens of power and politics:

in terms of struggles over meaning, the lived experience of paradox comes to life as imbued with power. Moreover, such struggles reveal dialectical tensions linked to the interplay of control and resistance, dominance and subordination, democracy and autocracy, empowerment and disempowerment, all rooted in discursive processes of clashing of thoughts, category work, ambiguity, bodies at work, and the like. (Fairhurst, 2022: 7)

Interpretatively, democracy and capitalism are perceived as being complementary and dialectically related.[1] In terms of complementarity, they share a number of elements. Both stress human agency; each relies on the rule of the law. They both reject ascribed status and depend on a 'shackled state' (Acemoglu and Robinson, 2019). Yet the two also are dialectically opposed: capitalism is globally cosmopolitan; democracy is tied to national territory; capitalism means one share unit is the currency of one vote, whereas in democracy it is one citizen who is entitled to one vote. There are challenges associated with the coexistence of these two processes: wealth may buy power, turning democracy into plutocracy; demagogues may seize or usurp power in the name of 'the people', assuming a populist role, turning democracy into autocracy. Democracy is a system of social cooperation via individual competition and consent; capitalism is a system of economic competition via organizationally framed cooperation and consent.

The debate on whether paradoxes exist in the realm of the real or in social constructions of what is taken to be real, remains a central focus. Smith and Lewis (2011) argue that the dualism of choice implicit in a social construction versus an inherent approach is not in itself paradoxical if one has to opt for one view or the other. They argue that paradoxes are *both* inherent *and* socially constructed. Paradoxes exist within systems that are real and are socially constructed through actors' cognition and rhetoric (Smith and Lewis, 2011). Hahn and Knight (2021) interrogated Smith and Lewis's arguments. Hahn and Knight (2021) articulate a hybrid view of paradoxes, using a metaphor from quantum physics. They propose that paradoxes exist as an inherent propensity, but do so in a latent probabilistic state that only becomes salient (thus real and enacted in a specific context) through 'observation', which makes them both inherent, as always already there, while also being latent. To become manifest, they must be socially constructed.

Paradoxes: latent, salient or both?

Inherent tensions can be triggered and come into being, meaning that they can be latent or salient. Central to paradox theory is the issue of whether the tensions that underlie paradox are inherent or socially constructed. It is possible that a paradox that is salient in one part of the organization is latent in another. Similarly, paradox will

---

[1]Wolf, M. (2023) 'In defence of democratic capitalism', *Financial Times*, 21–2 January 2023, pp. 1–2. Available at: www.ft.com/content/877d1a2d-67df-46a4-a3af-8e28198b944a

vary for different organizational members. What is salient for employees might not be for leaders. Paradoxes appear differently in different parts of an organization, depending on the interactional setting. One may suppress comments about some absurd request in front of one's boss while using irony to refer to it inside one's team (Jarzabkowski and Lê, 2017). For example, in the USSR, while jokes (*anekdoty*) against the system circulated abundantly, they did so in spaces in which telling jokes was accepted (after official meetings or during a class break); in other spaces (during an official meeting or during the class) they were dangerous for one's well-being. In other words, latency or salience could be chosen (Lempiälä et al., 2022). Paradox can thus be viewed as an interactional resource that actors can activate or deactivate depending on their particular context and interest. People may see paradox as a verb rather than a noun – something that people do rather than something that is seen as an attribute of a situation (Cunha et al., 2024).

Beyond the basic assumptions as to whether or not paradoxes are inherent or constructed, we now discuss the paradoxical attributes of latency and saliency. Paradoxes that are embedded in organizations may well remain latent (Smith and Lewis, 2011). Untriggered, their dormancy awaits detection (Tuckermann, 2019); hence, their recognition cannot be taken for granted (Knight and Paroutis, 2017). From a managerial perspective, latency lacks managerial appeal because non-issues remain resolutely elusive: that which is unseen and seemingly inert holds little appeal for managerial strategy. Characterizing the interpretivist view, organizational members make sense of perceived paradox (Tuckermann, 2018) and construct it as such (Putnam et al., 2016). In practice, the construction of a tension as either a paradox or non-paradox will be central as a matter of recognition (Jarzabkowski and Lê, 2017). Thus, latent tensions may become salient when triggered through cognition (Smith and Tushman, 2005) or in conditions of scarcity, plurality and change (Smith and Lewis, 2011), when the assumptions of normalcy are challenged.

Triggers enact awareness and experience of paradox on the part of organization members and how they approach/frame/problematize and respond to salient paradoxes. Salient paradoxes, therefore, are those that are consciously observed and articulated. In other words, tensions that underlie paradoxes remain latent until they are observed, and they become salient when they are enacted by a measurement apparatus (Hahn and Knight, 2021).

During COVID-19, the use of digital technologies intensified to unprecedented levels, so much so that the whole notion of physical space became questioned, especially in knowledge-based firms. The boundary that separated home and work dissolved as a result, making the work–life paradox central to many obliged to work from home (Pradies et al., 2021). The move to digitalized workplaces changed the nature of where people worked. As Kokshagina and Schneider (2023: 130) note:

[F]or many individuals and organizations around the world, the COVID-19 pandemic has not only accelerated the adoption of digital technologies but also paved the way for a lasting transformation of work, leveraging the efficiency and effectiveness gains those digital technologies offer. The virtual working environment has become a norm.

With the extraordinary adoption of digital technologies came new paradoxes. While the digital workplace has increased high levels of flexibility, it has also created the pressure to be in a constant state of connectivity and availability (Kokshagina and Schneider, 2023: 3). As a result, Harari (2014: 99) quipped that innovations meant to be time-saving – hence, making people's lives more relaxed – have instead made people more anxious and agitated:

> previously it took a lot of work to write a letter, address and stamp an envelope, and take it to the mailbox. It took days or weeks, maybe even months, to get a reply. Nowadays I can dash off an email, send it halfway around the globe, and (if my addressee is online) receive a reply a minute later. I've saved all that trouble and time, but do I live a more relaxed life? Sadly not. Back in the snail-mail era, people usually only wrote letters when they had something important to relate. Rather than writing the first thing that came into their heads, they considered carefully what they wanted to say and how to phrase it. They expected to receive a similarly considered answer. Most people wrote and received no more than a handful of letters a month and seldom felt compelled to reply immediately. Today I receive dozens of emails each day, all from people who expect a prompt reply. We thought we were saving time; instead we revved up the treadmill of life to ten times its former speed and made our days more anxious and agitated.

Final note

In this chapter, we covered two important and interrelated topics: philosophical roots and basic assumptions of paradoxes. In the West, paradoxes are viewed as abnormalities to be avoided, and solutions are based on differentiation and a non-contradictory approach, whereas in the East, paradoxes are embraced and seen as opportunities for creativity and innovation, with a tendency towards both/and thinking. Eastern philosophical traditions of Buddhism, Confucianism and Taoism view paradoxes as the norm, rather than an exception. They embed an accommodation of contradictions. The Afrocentric view in relation to paradoxes based on Ubuntu is an indigenous African way of sense-making based on humanness, harmony and continuity. In class, one exercise could be to share students' experience of paradoxes from their culture. An assignment could ask students to research different traditions in the way that they deal with paradoxes, mapping different approaches.

In addition to the philosophical roots, we also highlighted how we can approach paradoxes from two different perspectives: as objective realities where paradoxes exist in organizations or as subjective interpretations that emerge from social interactions – or both. You may ask why does it matter which epistemologies we adopt? We would answer that it matters because our predispositions affect how we recognize and respond to paradoxes. Depending on our ontological and epistemological views, we can better understand the conditions that make paradoxes more or less visible and salient. Theoretically, having a clear perspective helps us to explain how and why paradoxes arise and vary in different contexts.

5

Responding to Organizational Paradoxes

In this chapter, we will cover different responses to paradox at individual and organizational levels. For simplicity, we will present the responses as active and defensive. In addition, we will explore the dynamics of responses and how they change through time and across different levels of analysis. The responses will become more complex as we develop the argument. We begin by outlining the different ways in which organizational actors respond, and explain the difference between active and defensive responses.

In the previous chapters, we covered how responses, in general, are tied to the ways in which competing demands are problematized. Depending on how one problematizes tensions that emanate from competing demands, a response can be active, defensive, as well as a combination of both. Generally, tensions can be tackled by different organizational actors in more or in less integrative ways. Consider the following case:

Companies perceive paradoxical tensions in delivering greater accountability for deforestation events while maintaining a competitive supply base; and in transforming industry-wide problems through collective action while maintaining a competitive edge and respecting anti-trust law. As a result, firms resort to a wide range of responses that imply vastly different sustainability consequences. While creative approaches may help resolve emerging paradoxes, defensive approaches and the ignorance of tensions stand to further undermine progress toward zero-deforestation supply chains. (Grabs and Garrett, 2023).

In this case, material consequences attach to how the paradoxical tension is approached and dealt with.

The organizational context also matters when it comes to possible actions, as some organizations constitute favourable contexts to assume and manage tensions, whereas in other contexts, in the same sector, with generally similar overall conditions, contradictions are defied or given only lip service. When faced with competing demands, organizational actors can adopt different ways to deal with the resulting tension. The easy way may initially not be to deal with the tensions at all or to pretend that there is no tension. Second, organizational actors can decide to go with what they consider to be the correct or most favoured option. Third, organizational actors might decide to retain basic elements of both demands and attempt reconciliation. Fourth, actors might transcend the opposition and find a creative way that leads to synergy (Peng and Nisbett, 1999; Poole and Van de Ven, 1989).

Active vs defensive responses

In organization and management studies, Jarzabkowski et al. (2013) and Smith and Lewis (2011) categorized responses to competing demands as defensive and active, based on foundational works, such as Smith and Berg (1987), Vince and Broussine (1996) and Lewis (2000). Defensive responses aim at removing or 'solving' tension, while active responses attempt to harness tension and open up a space for a synergy (Gaim et al., 2022b). In defensive responses, the source of discomfort might initially disappear (Lewis and Smith, 2022), but comfort is fleeting and illusory as the result might be unintended consequences. Sometimes tensions are addressed via 'deparadoxification', the process of rendering salient paradoxes latent by hiding or concealing them in ways that they no longer need to be addressed. As a strategy to handle the issue of undecidability, if defensive approaches suppress the contradictory elements, deparadoxification conceals them (Schneckenberg et al., 2023).

Unanticipated consequences are common in business. Focusing on short-term financial benefit at the expense of long-term sustainability of a company may lead to collapse, as illustrated by FTX (see Box 2.1). Simplification of complexity may be problematic, even damaging for organization outcomes, leading to diminished attention to relevant issues and reduced organizational effectiveness (Carmine and De Marchi, 2023). An issue does not disappear just because one ignores it. Yet, in some cases, that is the kind of magical thinking evident in either/or forms of thinking. Suppression, though, is no solution.

In an active response, organizational members tap into paradoxes' potential as they are comfortable with accommodating the tension rather than resolving it once and for all, or at least they manage to accept the discomfort to generate creative outcomes from paradoxical challenges, seeing the tension as an opportunity for learning and growth (Rubin et al., 2023). In this way, paradoxical frames can promote integrative thinking. 'Acknowledging tensions may allow decision makers to achieve competing values simultaneously' (Hahn et al., 2018: 235).

People need to feel that they receive enough support in using paradoxes as opportunities for learning (Kahn, 2004). In the absence of such support, defensive responses are more likely. Hence, active responses entail long-term relief and sustainability (Smith and Lewis, 2011), unlike defensive responses, offering quick fixes. Table 5.1 distinguishes active from defensive responses.

Table 5.1   Active vs defensive responses

	Defensive responses	Active responses
Emotional reaction	Anxiety and defensiveness	Acceptance and comfort
Cognitive frame	'Either/or' thinking	'Both/and' thinking
View on resources	Limited	Abundant
Limits	Pulling paradoxical forces apart is futile – they are intertwined, locked in a persistent relationship	Not every tension is a paradox – integrating independent forces could be a waste of time
Behavioural manifestations of responses	Suppression, splitting, choosing	Synthesis, transcendence

Central to defensive/active responses are emotional reactions (Pradies, 2022; Vince and Broussine, 1996), cognitive frames (Miron-Spektor et al., 2011; Miron-Spektor et al., 2018), organizational actors' views of resources (Smith and Lewis, 2011), as well as a multitude of organizational conditions (Berti and Simpson, 2021) reflected in the behavioural manifestations summarized in Table 5.1.

Emotional reactions As highlighted above, when confronted with competing demands once a tension is made salient, although it is not a linear process, the emotional reaction of organization members can vary from emotional composure to the anxiety of having to deal with the absurd (Cunha et al., 2023a; Lewis, 2000). While in the face of paradox, some feel discomfort, emotional pressure and frustration, others feel encouraged to work through tensions (Beech et al., 2004; Patrick, 2018; Smith and Berg, 1987), in some cases, even seeming to enjoy them, as in the excitement and challenges of new start-ups (Cunha et al., 2023b). When paradox is considered to be a source of progress and fresh perspectives, it potentially becomes generative (Cunha et al., 2023a).

Cognitive frames Defensive responses are characterized by 'either/or' thinking in which competing demands are treated as mutually exclusive, functioning independently of each other (Smith and Lewis, 2011). Active responses are characterized by 'both/and' thinking. Both/and thinking implies developing cognitive capability to accommodate contradictions, learning to recognize, accept and profit from engaging the interdependent competing demands (Martin, 2007; Smith and Lewis, 2011).

View of resources The view that resources are scarce and limited might push actors to opt for defensive responses. However, recognizing that resources are abundant, not scarce, opens up the space for more active responses (Smith et al., 2016). When resources are limited, organizational actors' imagination is restricted with a focus that is more concerned with sharing the existing small pie or trying to have a bigger cut of it at another's expense. When resources are abundant, focus can turn to increasing the size of the pie.

Those who view resources as limited focus on the available options (on what is), while those who view resources as abundant focus on creating new possibilities (what could be; Gaim and Wåhlin, 2016). In practice, this involves competitors collaborating in coopetition (Raza-Ullah et al., 2014). For example, when Samsung collaborated with Sony to develop LCD in 2004, they sought to increase the size of the pie rather than struggling to gain a bigger slice of the existing pie (Gnyawali and Park, 2011).

As shown in Table 5.1, how organizational actors respond to competing demands (active and defensive) depends on a multitude of factors (the next chapter discusses the factors involved). Note that we are not indicating a positive or negative connotation to these responses, as the names might imply. Defensive responses can be strategic moves, in that sticking to one demand (for example, form over function), might be a source of competitive advantage (see Berti and Cunha, 2023; also see Box 5.1).

Behavioural manifestations in responding

Behavioural manifestations involve concrete steps and actions (Denison et al., 1995) materializing cognitive and emotional elements in individuals' responses within an organizational context. Grouped as 'defensive responses', some behavioural manifestations would be denial, regression, repression, projection (Jarzabkowski and Lê, 2017; Vince and Broussine, 1996), ambivalence (Lewis, 2000), spatial and temporal separation (Poole and Van de Ven, 1989). Vince and Broussine (1996) identified four defensive mechanisms. Repression blocks unpleasant experience from memory; regression refers to resorting to action that previously provided some security; projection denotes transferring personal shortcomings to others; reaction formation signifies refusal to accept an unpleasant reality (Vince and Broussine, 1996: 5).

Organizational actors assume multiple roles and have various interests which lead them to experience ambivalence, stemming from the simultaneous wish to be both 'a part' of the group and 'apart' from the group. Organizational actors can respond to tensions by resisting or by being unwilling fully to explore painful and distressing aspects of their experience (Smith and Berg, 1987: 211–12). They might attempt to eliminate tension by pitting members' opposing reactions against each other to see which proves stronger or more powerful (Smith and Berg, 1987: 212). Organizations can fail to recognize tension by 'putting aside' polarizing differences (Smith and Berg, 1987: 213–14) or assuming one pole while neglecting the other. For example, irrespective of climate change concerns, 'oil companies are "set to maximize returns to their shareholders and they're doing exactly that"'.[1] In another domain, prisons may be said to have a double mission with a paradoxical facet (Wenzel et al., 2019): to incarcerate and to educate, or to punish and rehabilitate. But 'pure, hard penal populism' is sometimes favoured – for instance, gang members are given less space than livestock at some of El Salvador's prisons.[2]

Separation-based responses leave assumptions about competing demands intact, considering that each pole of the paradox either operates at a different level (spatial separation) or is concentrated in a specific period of time (temporal separation) (Poole and Van de Ven, 1989: 566). Another manifestation of a defensive response can be seeking a middle ground, to make the tension seemingly disappear (Smith and Berg, 1987: 212). Attempts to compromise, eliminate and overlook, when integration is possible, mean missed opportunities to capitalize on possibilities at the intersection of competing demands. Let's now turn to active responses.

Grouped as 'active responses', some behavioural manifestations include synthesis (Poole and Van de Ven, 1989), transcendence (Abdallah et al., 2011; Lewis, 2000), and adjusting (Jarzabkowski et al., 2013). For example, in their book, *Creating Great Choices*, Riel and Martin (2017) give an excellent example of transcending paradoxes during the making of *The Lego Movie*. Jorgen Knudstorp, the CEO, had one project: to make a great film. There were two competing demands and choosing one meant losing out on the benefits of the other. He was challenged by the tension between maintaining total creative control and letting Hollywood have full control. Each had merit but neither was better.

With the first option, it meant that he had to hire screen writers and directors to execute a plan based on a corporate vision, a choice that would deter top-tier talent as it would be too confining for creative teams. The second would be letting Hollywood have full control, meaning that it would attract great talent but put the brand at risk. Instead of choosing one over the other, what Jorgen did was reframe the challenge. He connected the creative team with extreme Lego super fans and made the film makers embrace the Lego brand the way fans did. He required the creative team to spend time with Lego's super fans (kids and adults), to attend conventions, read letters, spend time with Lego employees, visit Lego stores. They had to soak up the culture.

The paradox in this case was not paralysing but rather energizing (Beech et al., 2004; Gaim and Wåhlin, 2016), in large part because Knudstorp Jorgen did not focus on contracts and legally binding documents. Although there were many options based on choice and compromises, he opted for creative integration and transcendence. Thus, when paradoxes are presented as exciting challenges, organization members break boundaries, embrace contradictions and unlock their creative energy (Carlsen et al., 2012a). Transcendence can be used to see a problem from a different perspective. This can be discussed from

---

[1] Wilson, T. and Brower, D., 'Big oil: Still profits before planet', *Financial Times*, 11–12 February 2023, p. 6.

[2] Murray, C. and Smith, A., 'Inside El Salvador's mega-prison: the jail giving inmates less space than livestock', *Financial Times*, 7 March 2023, p. 4. Available at: www.ft.com/content/d05a1b0a-f444-4337-99d2-84d9f0b59f95

the perspective of family businesses. It is usually said that paradoxes characterize the family–business relationship in the family firm, the two fundamentally distinct communicative spaces of the family and the business existing in a permanent state of tension. There are two markedly different logics of love and money at work.

Family businesses can be observed as families *or* as businesses, as *both*, as *neither* (Kleve et al., 2020). In the first cases, one perspective is favoured. In the both/and perspective, the two logics are juxtaposed. The two domains overlap. In the neither perspective, the two systems are not integrated. The two systems (family and business) in this perspective do not form one system, but rather the coupling of two independent systems. Observational paradox is deparadoxified via temporalization that observes the system as business and then as family. They can also be approached from a fifth position as in a tetralemma: switching from one problem/dilemma to another, such as representing family members as individuals with political positions. This may reframe the problem and perhaps help to find some new approach to a problem. When the logic is reframed and the offspring are viewed as qualified professionals for whom the prospect of returning to Mum and Dad is not 'very sexy',[3] the problem is perceived differently.

Leaders also engage in several activities to materialize active responses, such as making paradoxes visible so as to transcend them. In Cirque du Soleil, the founder (Guy Laliberté) saw that the company was leaning towards the corporate, forgetting creativity and art by focusing more on profitability and corporate efficiency. To bring the profitability–creativity, efficiency–art tension to the forefront, he brought a clown into the board room: Madam Zazou (Gregersen, 2017). She participated in the meetings of the board and made fun of the participants. What Laliberté did was playfully bring in the corporate–creativity tension for the top management team to recognize.

Henning Larsen, a Danish architecture firm, introduced a new role they call 'constructing architect'. It was designed to create a space for reconciliation between engineers and architects with opposing values and priorities in architectural projects. The constructing architect role is to serve as a third person and make sure that one side does not dominate the other, that the interdependence between the two ways of seeing is exploited. Thus, the third person serves as a bridge between architects and engineers, and makes sure that multiple voices are heard (Gaim, 2018). In other studies of multinational companies, researchers have identified the central role of supporting actors in moving from one framing/response (vicious cycle) to the other (virtuous cycle). These supporting actors are insiders to the organization but outsiders to the paradox (Pradies et al., 2021: 1242). We now turn our attention to voluntary and forced moves in the ways that organization members respond to competing demands.

Voluntary vs forced choices

As illustrated in Box 5.1, responses based on either/or thinking can be a *voluntary* and *rational choice*. Such a choice can be made as a matter of competitive

---

[3] Hill, A., 'Family firms: The succession trap', *Financial Times*, 13 March 2023, p. 15.

advantage. Making a free choice in the face of competing demands can also be a matter of optimization, meaning there is a condition of decidability (Berti and Cunha, 2023). For example, consider the many effective family firms that have out-lived many corporations through non-paradoxical strategies based on continuity, maintaining control in the traditional owners (Berti and Cunha, 2023).

Box 5.1 Noma: either/or choice as a competitive advantage

Noma was an innovative restaurant in Copenhagen, Denmark, whose head chef, René Redzepi, was known for his creativity and founding a new style of Scandinavian cui-sine. Heavily booked in advance, diners would have to spend close to US $500 (3,500 DKK) for a meal lasting a minimum of two to three hours, without juice or wine pair-ings included in the price.

Over the past 20 years, Noma's staff grew to over one hundred. The only thing that was mundane in Noma was its creativity, in which the 'pursuit of knowledge, devout creativity, relentless teamwork, and surprising our guests are essential to who we are'. Noma was named the world's best restaurant four times and was known for its use of unpaid interns, known as *stagiaires*. As a *Financial Times* writer noted, even though the restaurant was known for its use of natural ingredients, 'its employment model does not feel half as sustainable. Even diners who can afford it may think twice about flying long distances to be served elaborate meals that rely on low-paid chefs working long hours for perfection'.[4]

Unique items in the menu included 'spears of asparagus intentionally coated in white mold, and duck brains, and reindeer penis, and live shrimp that wriggled down your throat, and scatterings of a bracing spice that turned out to be ants'.[5] It was known not only for the highest quality of food, but for the standard it created for fine dining and training the finest chefs, spreading its ideas and values.[6] Thus, René Redzepi's choice of aesthetics over other demands (e.g., commercial demands) was a strategic choice. Choices, however, have consequences. Changing labour regulations meant the end of the unpaid *stagiaires*, making the operation commercially unviable. René Redzepi, as Noma closed its doors, said: 'fine dining at the highest level, with its gruelling hours and intense workplace culture, has hit a breaking point: it's unsustain-able'.[7] Executing consistently at a high level might not be easy, regardless of the initial success.

---

[4]Available at: https://www.ft.com/content/6377b292-d825-4b3a-8527-04d1475511b0
[5]Available at: www.esquire.com/food-drink/food/a42476466/noma-copenhagen-closing-stagiaires/
[6]Available at: www.theguardian.com/commentisfree/2023/jan/24/noma-is-closing-are-we-seeing-the-death-of-fine-dining
[7]Available at: www.nytimes.com/2023/01/09/dining/noma-closing-rene-redzepi.html

Similar to Noma (Box 5.1), yet with different outcomes are Japanese *shinise*, in which preserving tradition in a family business is a source of balance. *Shinise* are companies, including restaurants, typically run by the same families for decades, following the same organizational logic sustained via balancing *both* tradition *and* modernity. Tradition is invested in as a source of differentiation (see https://kyotofoodie.com/category/shinise/) and the original core business (the element of tradition) does not change (Krahnke et al., 2018). However, each *shinise* is different and relevant because it expresses a community individually.

Noma and *shinise* may be extraordinary exemplars but regarding the latter, think about your city: there will certainly be organizations that play a more or less similar role, business firms that trade on tradition, its authenticity and longevity. They seem to have existed forever. For this reason, they are not just businesses but pillars of a community. In fact, being embedded in a *community* is the reason for their longevity. One of us lives in a mainly Italian Sicilian neighbourhood in Sydney, Australia. Restaurants come and go, but the Italian ones that go, go very quickly. Word passes around in the 'nonna' network, at the school gates, after mass, as to which restaurants respect tradition and produce excellent food and have authentic staff. The tradition is kept alive by the community.

Forced choice takes different forms. Decision in the face of competing demands entails either a choice of one thing at the expense of another (i.e., as a dilemma) or some form of reconciliation (i.e., as trade-offs). When a forced choice is made, it might lead to temporary relief as the tension is 'resolved' (Smith and Lewis, 2011); however, relief is short-lived. The need for the other will come back or be exacerbated (Sundaramurthy and Lewis, 2003), launching a vicious cycle. A vicious cycle can be explained by the following example. When the consequences of government budget cuts and interest rate rises reduces spending, in the long run, as recession sours the economy, the government receives less revenue because fewer people are employed and there are fewer transactions to be taxed. Budget cuts lead to various assistance programmes and unemployment benefits being terminated. The increased need for assistance and benefits and the administration thereof further necessitates increased cuts. Yet any cut is followed by increased pay-outs and other assistance programmes. Thus, doing one at the expense of the other leads to a vicious cycle.

In forced choices, 'conditions of undecidability prevail and neither of the alternative poles can be neglected without causing a rationality breakdown' (Berti and Cunha, 2023), leading to a choice of unsustainable outcomes (Smith and Lewis, 2011). When actors lack agency or access to resources to deal with the mutually irreconcilable, what are called pragmatic paradoxes ensue (Berti et al., 2021). Pragmatic paradoxes lead to confusion and powerlessness, with people confronted with requests that are absurd (Berti et al., 2021). In other cases, organization actors resort to impression management and deception (Gaim et al., 2021) or are left paralysed because they can't negotiate the competing demands (Cunha et al., 2023a).

When actors can explore synergy and are stimulated to search for a way to accommodate both demands, they are said to transcend the paradox or, as Abdallah et al. (2011) would put it, having their cake and eating it too. In this case, paradoxes are generative and are treated as unavoidable situations that can potentially originate positive outcomes (Berti and Cunha, 2023).

Adaptive responses

Organizational members' responses to competing demands and the resulting tensions are not stable, nor is their problematization (Gaim et al., 2022). Moreover, dealing with organizational tensions can be precarious in that organizational members who responded generatively, via active responses, might return to past practices that can undo the active response (Luscher and Lewis, 2008). Thus, organizational actors changing the way they make sense of competing demands do so through increased understanding (Raisch et al., 2018) or establishing coping practices (Gaim et al., 2022) to deal with the tension or new pressures.

In practice, organizational actors can change their problematization and reframe competing demands as paradoxes, when they were initially framed as dilemmas, if external actors intervene (Gaim et al., 2018). For example, action research carried out by Luscher and Lewis (2008) shows that organization members can work through competing demands by altering their framing as a result of collaborative intervention. Similarly, Pradies et al. (2021) conducted action research in a multinational energy company and showed how actors moved between vicious and virtuous cycles as they dealt with competing demands, given the many contextual conditions that influence management practices. More specifically, the authors identified three practices undertaken to enable a progressive shift such as: '(1) breaking dysfunctional dynamics to disrupt the vicious cycle; (2) facilitating new responses to enable cycle reversal; and (3) embedding virtuous dynamics in the organization' (Pradies et al., 2021: 1258). Beyond cognition and behaviour, the authors show how the environment in which organizational actors operate either helps or prevents meaningful shifts from vicious to virtuous cycles. Similar to third parties that bridge competing forces (Gaim, 2018), Pradies et al. (2021: 1259) demonstrate the relevance of those 'who are insiders to the organization yet outsiders to the paradox' in helping others to shift their framing and response.

Berti and Cunha (2023) developed what they call a double loop model of paradox. A double loop model involves an iterative process and multiple attempts to deal with competing demands. These demands arise from a multitude of factors changing the framing of tensions adaptively as a process. Organizational actors change their framing of organizational tensions as they learn about their nature and increase their understanding, as well as their practices in the process. Thus, adaptive responses, unlike linear responses, reflect reality. The dynamic is similar to that of jazz. Those who follow adaptive responses act as do good jazz improvisers – they 'excel at both exerting their power and relinquishing it at the appropriate time' (Greer et al., 2023). They do so creatively, improvising with the evolving flow.

Weak vs strong paradoxes

When organization actors decide to engage competing demands as paradoxes, there is an implicit assumption that such paradoxes are equal across time and space. In reality, not all paradoxes are equal – paradoxes vary in terms of how they are experienced. As highlighted above, employees with different cultural backgrounds might experience paradoxes differently (Keller et al., 2017).

Work–life balance (see Box 5.2) as a paradox is experienced differently by the same person. An employee that was previously without parental responsibilities will see balance differently when they become a parent with responsibilities for children. Different people, in similar life situations, will also have diverse work–life paradox experiences related to their access to resources (Gaim et al., 2022). Gender is an important contextual consideration not only in differences in life and living, but also in the availability and accessibility of resources during different phases of life. In general, while both men and women can face similar paradoxes, normative expectations make the experience of the work–life paradox more intense for females (Padavic et al., 2020), that are often putting in a 'double-shift' (Baxter et al., 2008) of unpaid domestic as well as paid employment duties. In this example, those with access to more resources have many more options to lessen the intensity of the work–life paradox by the simple expedient of hiring others to do the home life work – the housework. Thus, considering not only the simultaneity and interdependence of contradictory demands but also their intensity can enrich the conceptualization of paradox.

Mundane vs remarkable paradoxes

Some paradoxes are mundane in the way they are navigated, while others are remarkable. We will discuss mundanity first, illustrated through two examples: in social enterprises, where paradox is entrenched in both being profitable and making a positive social impact (Gümüsay et al., 2020; Smith and Besharov, 2019), dealing with this paradox will be mundane, a part of everyday working life.

There are also situations in which dealing with paradox becomes the principal *raison d'être*. Recall Gaim's (2018) reporting on the role of a construction architect in a Danish architectural firm, Henning Larsen, serving as a third person bridging professional relations between architects and engineers. The construction architect's role is 'to make sure one side (either poetics or techne) does not dominate the other and that the interdependence between these competing forces is sufficiently exploited. The third person facilitates and makes sure that multiple voices are heard' (Gaim, 2018: 507). Thus, navigating paradox is a mundane and regular part of the job for the construction architect.

In architecture, there are moments when contradictions transcend the mundane in an aesthetic moment (Gaim et al., 2022; Palmer and Dunford, 2002). Perhaps the greatest example of this, as we discussed in Chapter 2, is Frank Gehry's remarkable Guggenheim Museum in Bilbao, built in a declining industrial port on the site of derelict port facilities, creating a masterpiece of design, capable of not only lifting the spirits with its grace and boldness, but also the economy of the Basque region.

Navigating paradox can also be remarkable. As reported by Abdallah et al. (2011), closure of hospitals led to improved healthcare – something seemingly against the norm and hence paradoxical.

Here is a case that illustrates a creative twist that would be characterized as the transcendence of paradox. In 2014's comedy special 'All Over the Map!', a famous American ventriloquist, Jeff Dunham, ran into trouble. After booking a show in

Malaysia, he was approached by the Ministry of Arts, History and Culture and was told, politely but strictly, not to bring Achmed the Dead Terrorist, one of his notable dummies, on stage. Local sensitivities were significant despite Jeff Dunham's show of the Achmed the Dead Terrorist being one of the most viewed videos in YouTube's history. Instructed not to mention the name or any reference to Achmed the Dead Terrorist, he had to omit any references to anything remotely related to religion, refraining from saying the name 'Achmed' or mentioning a certain virgin birth. Jeff Dunham was worried about the audience as they may well have come to see Achmed, given that the show was promoted with Achmed on the poster.

With the ban, Jeff Dunham had to accommodate multiple demands, that of the audience, the state and his artistry. He had to be creative and find a way to respect the host country's law, while maintaining the integrity of his artistry and pleasing the audience that had paid to see the famous dummy. So instead of 'Achmed the Dead Terrorist', he brought his brother 'Jacques Merde the Dead French Terrorist', equipped with a moustache and beret. Before introducing his 'new' dummy, Jeff Dunham said, 'I want to respect the request 'cause I am a guest here but at the same time you paid your money to see what you thought you were going to see – that certain person is not here. However, his brother is here. He is from France.' After the show, Jeff Dunham said, 'I don't want to go too far to be offensive, but at the same time I have to because that is what got me here.' Some transcending responses require risky out-of-the-box thinking.

While dealing with paradoxes can be mundane, in other instances it can give rise to paradoxes that are managed remarkably (see also the case of Lego earlier in this chapter).

Box 5.2 Work-life balance

Work–life balance means managing the competing demands of work and personal lives. Depending on many existentially individual conditions, the challenge of balancing work and life can be different, even for those working the same job in the same organization. The balance between work and life may also change at different times in our lives and involve choices, struggle and guilt, manifested in many forms.

- What does turning down a social invitation say about my work commitments?
- Do I have to choose between my child's recital or attending a weekend workshop?
- How will I take care of personal responsibilities while spending long hours in the office?
- Why should I feel guilty that I am not giving 100 per cent to both work and family life?
- Will I end up burnt out trying to juggle both work and life?
- Should I be spending time on my hobbies while I should be working for that promotion?
- Should I focus on advancing my career or prioritizing my family?
- Why do I feel like I'm sacrificing my life for work? This question surfaced while one of us was editing this text late in the evening, alone in the office corridor and far from family.

(Continued)

> The same paradox can be experienced differently by different organizational members, something that became all too evident during the pandemic when people worked from home, some doing so easily, with no dependants or commitments while others, whose lives were enriched by these relations, would make a less easy transition.

In addition to *culture* and *normative expectations*, the experience of paradox also has to do with the very *nature of the organization*. Some organizations are designed for one predominant purpose. A typical organization might have a commercial purpose at the core of its operation with other demands being marginal. You go to work, work there and then go home – unless you are a Japanese salaryman (Cook, 2019), that is. After work, you are expected to go out drinking with your workmates and your boss, and are not expected to leave for home until your boss has left. If it is very late, you may not even go home; you may choose to sleep in a capsule hotel (see Figure 5.1), in one of many small capsules, piled on top of each other. The paradox is that work and life cannot easily be distinguished, so the idea of balance is paradoxical. A similar situation occurs in the top consulting companies where the norm is that you make your salary between 9 and 5, and your promotion between 5 and 9. Excessive work hours are, paradoxically, normal.

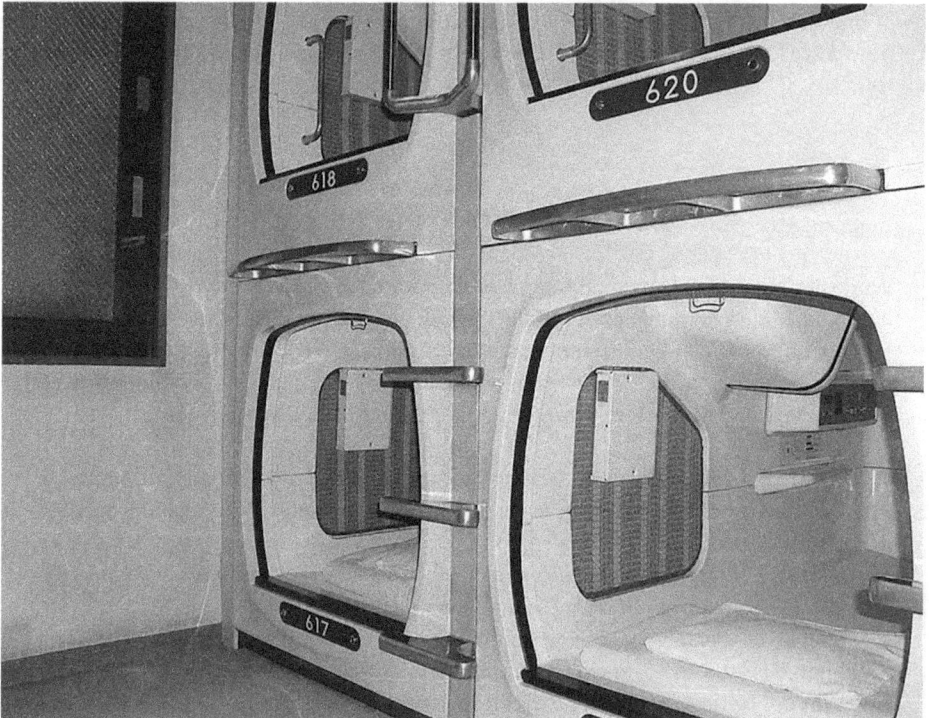

Figure 5.1   Capsule hotel

Source: Reproduced under the CC BY 2.0. License

In some other organizations characterized by hybridity (Smith and Besharov, 2019), such as social enterprises, in which commercial and social demands are integral parts of the operational and strategic operations, paradox is felt less intensely. Indeed, as organization actors implicitly navigate tensions, paradox can seem to be latent (Gümüsay et al., 2020). Incubate, a Muslim social incubator in Germany, was founded as a hybrid organization integrating religion, commerce and community. Incubate was not only a new organization, but it was also institutionally novel. Nothing like it had been seen previously; its members were unsure how to resolve the paradox of being religious and being commercial without causing offence to their community. The wider business community did not understand what they were trying to achieve. Their very existence appeared paradoxical.

Box 5.3   CSR strategy at top and operational levels: the case of child labour

Child labour is not only a huge issue in developing countries, it also presents many ethical dilemmas for companies operating in developed countries. Companies in developed countries have policies as part of their corporate social responsibility initiatives that ban the use of child labour.

It is easy to conceive of sustainability strategy at strategic level, but what does that mean to those who have to act on it? In principle, banning child labour is generally considered to be a positive step, as it can help to protect children from exploitation and abuse. However, it is important to recognize that in some cases, banning child labour can also have unintended consequences, such as leaving children and their families without a source of income. In situations where banning child labour could lead to children starving or facing other serious negative consequences, how should someone in the Indian subcontinent act, for example (see Khan et al., 2007)?

Paradoxes can also be experienced differently at different levels. The expectations of many members of organizations are that leaders' tasks will include resolving paradoxes so that routine organizational functioning can proceed smoothly. The expectation that leaders will approach paradox differently from other individual organizational members is frequently encountered in the literature. Moreover, there is a tendency to accept that the same paradox is experienced the same way throughout the organization and across its levels. For example, paradox can be experienced less intensely at the top, where it is formulated, than at the bottom, where its consequences must be tolerated.

Leaders deal with many paradoxes, such as *innovation paradoxes*, where new products and processes conflict with existing practices, and with *supply chain paradoxes* that involve tensions between local sourcing and boundary-crossing integration. *Obligation paradoxes* arise when the goal of maximizing profits for shareholders clashes with the desire to generate social impact benefits for stakeholders. Success in such situations depends on addressing conflicting demands simultaneously, not choosing between them (Smith et al., 2016). This is the essence of a both/and approach to dealing with paradoxes. Easy at the top, perhaps, but all strategy relies on practice, not design or top-level thinking. Practice relies on others as relays in a complex network of organization relations. By the time the network extension is reached at its perimeters, where the action is often located, both/anding may not be so clear. For example, the Theranos case (see Box 7.1) explains the paradoxical difference between the rhetoric at the top and the technological enigma at the bottom in practice. Thus, the intensity of experience associated with paradoxes can be very different, depending on the context in which a paradox becomes salient.

Final note

Although problematization matters in responding to tensions, in practice it is not stable. Organization actors change their problematization and thus their responses will be contingent on multiple organizational factors. These can include access to and the availability of resources, power dynamics, and existing organizational practices that have worked in dealing with the same problem in the past or elsewhere. Just because organizational actors are faced with competing demands does not necessarily mean that they have to accommodate them or engage in trade-offs. Choice is also an option both in the short and the long term. If you look back to Box 2.2, when an athlete competes in Muay Thai, they train for strength which is the reverse for those who specialize in Taekwondo. The same is true for those who want to compete in powerlifting vs bodybuilding – although both use weight training, the goal is distinct, thereby they have to make a choice. Moreover, trade-offs do not imply paradoxical choices (Berti and Cunha, 2023).

6

Boundary Conditions: What Does It Take to Deal with Paradoxes?

In this chapter, we will answer the question: 'What does it really take to deal with paradoxes?' In so doing, we will highlight the importance of not only a paradoxical mindset, but also the role of agency as organization members respond to contradictions. This chapter is particularly helpful in practising paradoxically. Although we have highlighted the importance of problematizing tensions as paradoxes and how responses are tied to problematization, there are also a multitude of factors that need to be considered for effectively practising paradoxes.

Beyond treating tensions that result from competing demands as an anomaly to be resolved by the 'right' choice, if one accepts paradoxes as opportunities to leverage tensions effectively, tapping into their potential, as shown in Pradies's (2022) work on emotion, it necessarily requires a 'paradoxical mindset', as highlighted by Miron-Spektor et al. (2018). However, a paradoxical mindset is in itself insufficient; Smith (2014) highlights enabling conditions while Gaim et al. (2022b) discuss boundary conditions. Moreover, the very concept of 'mindset' is either highly reductionist, given that having a mind is an irreducibly individual phenomenon, or it is a conflation that assumes that there can be a common collective consciousness. Any mindset must be partly relational: participating in heterogeneous networks facilitates more nuanced, paradoxical responses than participation in more homogeneous networks that increase the propensity to favour some specific pole (Keller et al., 2020). Any mindset is influenced by sociomaterial factors (Aoki, 2020). For example, the fact that Nokia favoured the use of the company's products by employees, combined with a lack of direct experience with customers, may have caused a lack of sensitivity to the threat coming from the iPhone: if you don't use it, you cannot feel it; if you cannot feel it, you can dismiss it (Vuori, 2023; Vuori and Huy, 2022). Companies can promote paradoxical responses via exposure to objects such as competitors' products, defective items, customer letters, etc. The famous episode of Zhang Ruimin breaking products at Haier (Wei, 2009) illustrates the need to include objects in the development of a paradoxical way of thinking: how to be *both* positive/hopeful *and* critical about one's organization. In 1985, Ruimin made his factory workers smash 76 defective refrigerators with sledgehammers, delivering the first blow himself. Defective quality was not to be tolerated was the message, communicated loud and clear. The case of Haier, the Chinese multinational, also illustrates the tension between discipline and tight controls for the germination of innovative contexts. As explained by Liu and Li (2002), a heavy managerial hand was necessary to create conditions for the innovative hub to flourish, as we know it today. In other words, strict discipline was necessary for the creation of an innovative company.

Working through paradoxes requires not only change in the orientations and dispositions of those individuals dealing with them, but it also changes the context in which these individuals and paradoxes are embedded. Thus, not only are appropriate 'mindsets' required; the necessary conditions (e.g., agency, access to resources, psychological safety) must be created if organization members are to deal with paradoxes. Managers have been urged to create environments rich in psychological safety, manifested as comfort with sharing mistakes, concerns and disagreements without fear of retribution. For psychological safety to work, however, it must be practised persistently ('leaders should "persistently praise" people who speak up', as pointed out by Skapinker[1]) and be tempered with other attributes, such as accountability or intellectual honesty. Consider the case of safety in situations in which there is an absence of intellectual honesty or accountability. What would you expect in terms of outcomes such as performance or creativity? Would safe working practices be those devoid of criticism, or would they be those that raised awkward issues that were organizationally off-limits as non-issues, given the prevailing hypocrisy? (Dyer et al., 2023; Edmondson, 2018).

Whether a paradox will be dealt with generatively or pathologically will depend on a host of factors. Of course, while these factors are interrelated, we will present them separately for ease of reading.

Mindset and emotional composure

Most of our discussion about responding to paradox has, as is typical in current theorizing, focused on whether organizational actors have the 'right mindset' (Miron-Spektor et al., 2011) and emotional reaction (Smith and Lewis, 2011).

---

[1] Skapinker, M., 'Why managers fail to plan for the worst-case scenario', *Financial Times*, 20 March 2023, p. 14.

Managers may support employees adopting a paradoxical mindset so as to see reality as complex and multifaceted through thinking and acting paradoxically (Boemelburg et al., 2023).

Yet mindset and emotional composure are only pieces of the puzzle. Those who are comfortable with inconsistencies, and who are composed when confronted with competing demands and are cognitively able to juxtapose competing demands, are better able to deal with paradoxes productively (Miron-Spektor et al., 2018). Yet even those who can juxtapose competing demands and are emotionally composed when confronting tension will be stifled if they are not authorized to exercise agency or secure access to resources (Berti and Simpson, 2021).

Agency and access to resources

Beyond the individual's emotional composure and mindset, engaging with paradoxes also requires agency and access to resources. Power relations inform and limit actors' capacity to deal with competing demands. If actors are not empowered to deal with paradoxes generatively, the experience of paradox will be a source of distress, with the competing pressures seeming to present a sense of absurdity (Berti and Cunha, 2023). If organizational actors are to engage in dialogical interactions to navigate paradoxes, 'they need a space that encourages interaction and the power to engage in dialogue with those who hold contradictory views' (Gaim et al., 2022a: 14).

In the case of the paradox of work–life balance, a working parent may be able to juggle multiple competing roles and be emotionally composed, if they have the ability to access resources that will enable them to deal productively with paradox, especially when the intensity of the paradox is high. It is often remarked that women with children are the world's best managers because they juggle so many competing responsibilities. They are even better managers if they have access to resources to enable them to do so successfully, such as affordable or free childcare, or an income that supports a nanny or au pair.

As was illustrated in Box 5.3, for those who ban child labour, knowing well that the children and their families may starve as a consequence, the response to the tension between what is legal and what is right can trigger negative emotions, such as frustration and anguish.

Organizational context

Some organizations might be more conducive to dealing with paradox generatively, given their values, routines and other organizational practices. By their very nature, social enterprises and other forms of hybrid organization have dual goals to maintain, meaning that paradox is ever present, not as an anomaly so much as an ordinary organizational function (Smith and Besharov, 2019). Thus, if effective coping practices are readily available, paradox can be navigated generatively (Gaim et al., 2022b).

For example, in another of our studies, an architectural firm created a role to help architects. In the Norwegian architectural firm, Snøhetta, which built the Oslo Opera House, every project group has someone called a 'groupie' who is invited to observe and listen to the team's ideas and reflections at regular intervals during the project period. This person is not part of the team per se, as he or she is supposed to provide the outsiders' view on the process. The groupie is expected to criticize, enrich and bolster ideas, as well as provide solutions for the creative process of the team (Carlsen et al., 2012b; Gaim et al., 2019).

Power asymmetry and degree of polarization

When actors are polarized and there is power asymmetry, more powerful actors can dominate one side of the polarity and silence the need of the other (Berti and Cunha, 2023). In a notable project – the Sydney Opera House – the two key actors – the architect (Jørn Utzon) and the engineer (Ove Arup) – became polarized as the ideation–execution paradox intensified, leading eventually to Utzon's forced resignation. The design for the project that he created was one for which he was to receive significant subsequent fame, but that never resulted in another significant commission. His dismissal from the project by the client organization, the New South Wales government, saw him represented as unable to deliver on time, on budget, or with designs that were buildable. What should have been a brilliant career was destroyed. The power dynamic was so polarized that it led to the dominance of a single engineering voice (with the ear of the government) and withdrawal of the other, depriving the project of the tension necessary for the paradox of ideation and execution to be a persistently generative force. Monological interactions resolved the paradox through silencing the blending of different voices, by exercising power over, rather than power with, the other (Gaim et al., 2022a: 13).

In another relevant example, the paradox between safety and commercial continuity (Pradies et al., 2021) was central during the COVID-19 pandemic; however, the polarity among politicians, as well as with publics, impeded dealing generatively with the pandemic because draconian responses, such as lock-downs, were met with stark opposition.

Box 6.1   Sheryl Sandberg and the myth of doing it all

In her book, *Lean In — Women, Work and the Will to Lead,* Sheryl Sandberg, the former Chief Operating Officer of Facebook, wrote about the myth of 'doing it all' or 'having it all', particularly as it relates to women and the balancing of work and family. Sandberg has noted that this myth is harmful because it sets an unrealistic standard for people to strive for, often leading to feelings of guilt and inadequacy when people are unable to meet this standard. The expectation that women should be able to manage their careers and their families without any support or help can create a feeling of isolation and of being overwhelmed, discouraging them from pursuing their career goals.

Instead of striving for the impossible goal of 'doing it all', Sandberg encourages people to focus on finding balance and making choices that are right for them. She advises people to be honest with themselves about their priorities, and to seek out the support and resources they need to manage their responsibilities effectively. Sandberg's message is that it is not necessary or even possible to have it all, and that it is more important to focus on finding happiness and fulfilment in *both* work *and* personal life. It is easier for professional women, of course; for working-class women in the gig economy or holding down more than one job, it is impossible. Context *is* very important.

Final note

In this chapter, we highlighted that sufficient agency is a necessary precondition for a paradoxical mindset to emerge and to deploy its effects. In addition, we presented how the availability of successful paradox-coping practices can affect an organization member's response to paradoxes. We have outlined the boundary conditions which, we hope, could make paradox theorizing more complex, and fill the gap between theory and practice. Moreover, outlining the boundary conditions helps to distinguish paradoxes that can be productively engaged and those that can be stifling, when engaged in certain conditions.

7

Here Comes Trouble: The Dark Side of Paradoxes

In this chapter, we will show some of the difficulties of managing paradoxes. When dealing with paradoxes, there are some unintended consequences that should make leaders cautious. We will show how leaders should pay attention to the gap between what they say about using paradoxes transcendentally and what transpires in practice. Moreover, what scholars say should be done must be interpreted with caution, as the theory–practice gap may be wide, which is another paradox.

Although there are many positive aspects of paradox theory, there are also critical voices. Gaim et al. (2021) issue cautions about the appeal of paradoxical objectives and how actors might engage in 'false mastery of paradox', while Berti and Simpson (2021) introduce the notion of 'pragmatic paradoxes', warning readers to be critical of recommendations in paradox theory that are insensitive to power inequalities. The concept of pragmatism here refers to the work of Paul Watzlawick and his colleagues (Watzlawick et al., 1967). Pragmatics is in this case the branch of linguistics that refers to language in use. Some uses of language confront people with impossible choices such as orders that need to be disobeyed to be obeyed or 'choices' without options; for cinema aficionados, there are 'offers that you cannot refuse'. Of course, these pragmatic paradoxes, such as some 'invitations' from some bosses, are not spaces for organizational dialogue and renewal, as pictured by mainstream organizational paradox theory. On the contrary, they are instantiations of organizational absurdity. As they illustrate, acceptance of 'both/and' solutions can neither be always possible nor desirable (Berti and Cunha, 2023).

Desirable but not possible

As illustrated by the case of Theranos (see Box 7.1) or the VW emissions scandal (see Box 7.5), both/and might be desirable but not possible. In both cases, the technology that would make blood testing or diesel engines *better*, *faster* and *cheaper* did not exist except in the imagination of the top-level managers in both Theranos (Tourish and Willmott, 2023) and VW (Gaim et al., 2021). Thus, pursuing an impossible paradoxical dream can indeed produce a costly disaster, as was evident in both cases. Pursuing a paradox that is impossible to achieve, such as that in Theranos, is a case of strategic quagmires, in which leaders 'overestimate their abilities [...] and think too highly of the likelihood of success' (Spicer, 2023: 342).

The world is full of examples of impossible paradoxes. These examples not only include greedy CEOs, but also normal leaders. Over time, different authors have created enough cases to allow the compilation of a list of demands that are interconnected but contradictory, confronting people with orders that can neither be refused nor obeyed, orders indicating pragmatic paradoxes. Consider the following cases:

- Take the initiative ... Don't break the rules.
- Before taking the initiative, you should ask my permission.
- You must give notice of your mistakes ... Mistakes will not be tolerated.
- Think long-term ... Deliver immediately!
- Cooperate ... Compete.
- Do learn from mistakes ... Do things right the first time.
- You need to be autonomous – we need more empowerment ... My decision is ...
- Show you are a good team player ... Your performance will be assessed through a forced-ranking system.
- Tell me what you think ... You must show respect (think about what you are going to say).
- You must save quality time to think ... but we will ask to fill all sorts of admin procedures.
- This team is experiencing lots of problems ... You should bring me solutions, not problems.
- This is a flexible workplace ... you can work any 15 hours you want.
- Our company's survival depends on laying off a third of our workforce. But no one will be fired. All departures will be agreed.
- Even when you feel sad, you must show a genuine smile to our customers.
- In the context of the COVID-19 pandemic, work should be remote as much as possible (written norm) ... Meetings of this committee should be presential (oral communication).

Box 7.1   Theranos and Elizabeth Holmes

From 'The next Steve Jobs' to 11 years of prison for fraud

Elizabeth Holmes dropped out of Stanford and founded Theranos when she was 19 years old to realize the idea of a blood test that could detect hundreds of diseases, while using only a single drop of blood. The technology was promised to be faster, cheaper and far better than existing options. In the process, the promise made Elizabeth Holmes one of the world's youngest self-made billionaires, with Theranos valued at US $9 billion. After failing to deliver the promised technology for almost 15 years, it was discovered that Theranos never had the technology in the first place. Holmes was sentenced to 11 years in prison for fraud after the promised technology was revealed to be a sham.

Why was the new technology so captivating?

The originality of the promised new technology was that it would deliver about 70 lab tests that could be run on just one drop of blood from a finger prick, not the usual full vial of blood. Moreover, the new technology would offer an opportunity to track the medical history of patients. The new technology could be described as a transcending solution to a paradoxical challenge. The technological promise was that it would be *faster, better* and *cheaper* than normal blood-testing. That promise was why Theranos was valued in the billions and the reason behind the countless awards and recognitions bestowed on its founder – at least initially.

Amid the success that Holmes was enjoying, there was only one problem. The promised product had never been peer reviewed – a gold standard in the industry. The lack of peer review and secrecy that characterized Theranos, as well as the failure to show how the technology worked, made outsiders, especially the scientific community, sceptical. Sceptical scientists were subsequently to talk to investigative journalists who reported that Theranos was using the technology of competitors after more than a decade of development because their core technology could not deliver what it promised.

Why did it take so long?

Twelve years into the development of the promised technology and the excitement around it, Theranos was not able to turn the enthusiasm into a concrete product. Theranos's focus had been on the narrative about the technology rather than the application of the technology. Typical to Silicon Valley's 'fake it until you make it' mentality, outsiders were taken in by the narrative of success and the glamour and excitement of the individuals 'around' the technology, rather than the technology itself. Before it even had a working prototype, Theranos was associated with influential investors, such as Timothy Draper and Don Lucas (a godfather-like figure in Silicon Valley), and Oracle CEO Lawrence Ellison. Theranos's board of directors also included famous senior government officials, a retired US Navy admiral, former US cabinet secretaries, a US Marine Corps general and two former senators, all of whom knew nothing about the technology or the industry.

For more on Theranos and Elizabeth Holmes, read John Carreyrou's (2018) book, *Bad Blood: Secrets and Lies in a Silicon Valley Startup*, or watch the HBO documentary *The Inventor: Out for Blood in Silicon Valley*, directed and produced by Alex Gibney.

Paradox is not easy to transcend; those who promise to have embraced paradoxical demands offering a product that is better, cheaper and faster have been caught out in organizational misbehaviour (see also Box 7.5 on VW emissions). Although captivating, transcending paradoxes is neither easy nor impossible, but rhetoric doesn't bridge that gap.

Elizabeth Holmes's overconfidence was a source of competitive advantage; however, convincing the world through words and delivering on promises, especially when they are material (such as a technology that must work), poses a problem. Overconfidence, according to Spicer (2023: 342), means that 'people make inaccurate judgement and commit themselves to questionable paths of action'.

In the big tech firms, such as Google, Meta and Twitter (after Elon Musk's takeover), 2022/23 saw a massive wave of large-scale job cuts. According to layoffs.fyi (a website that tracks layoffs in the tech industry) 160,997 employees were laid off in 2022 from 1,045 tech companies. On 22 February 2023, 392 tech companies had already laid off 108,901 employees. In April 2024, 229 tech companies laid off 57,505 employees. One thing that has been central during the 2022/23 layoffs has been to find a way to let go of employees in a way that shows compassion and understanding while achieving the objective that necessitated the layoff, which is often referred to as 'compassionate layoff'. Compassionate layoff has been pursued, but turned out to be an elusive goal.[1]

In fact, showing compassion at the time of layoffs could also manifest inhumanity. Trying hard to satisfy the competing needs of various stakeholders may lead to phoney compassion. One notable case has been 'the crying CEO' who sacked two people, then posted a weeping selfie on LinkedIn. The backlash to the post was swift as people picked up the fake compassion where he cried about firing two of seventeen employees at his marketing agency and turned their misfortune into a self-aggrandizing post (he seemed to be good at marketing because the post is still posted and he has edited his bio on LinkedIn at 'viral crying CEO'[2]). In any case, his compassionate layoff has backfired:

> People make fools of themselves on the internet every day. The reason this particular piece of content generated so much attention is that Wallake's performative empathy is a perfect encapsulation of everything that is irritating about LinkedIn and, by extension, everything that is wrong with corporate culture.[3]

(Mis)managing paradoxes and unintended consequences

As highlighted above, responding to competing demands through both/and is not for the faint-hearted. Moreover, multiple factors, both inside and outside of organizations, can disturb the balance. Thus, 'normalizing both-and can also trap actors in oppressive

[1]Available at: www.bbc.com/worklife/article/20230221-the-myth-of-the-compassionate-layoff
[2]Available at: www.theguardian.com/commentisfree/2022/aug/16/crying-ceo-sacked-two-people-selfie-linkedin
[3]Available at: www.theguardian.com/commentisfree/2022/aug/16/crying-ceo-sacked-two-people-selfie-linkedin

situations' (Berti and Cunha, 2023) in which achieving the desired outcome might be one thing, while maintaining it might prove extremely difficult. While the idea that balance is temporary and the organizations must be kept at the edge of chaos (Davis et al., 2009) is part of the intuitive appeal of the dynamic equilibrium model, it is necessary to consider that such a balance is precarious and fragile.

Owing to the pandemic, individuals, organizations and nations have had to deal with myriad paradoxes. Central has been the challenge of simultaneously protecting the economy while saving human life: attending to the short-term needs of saving lives while attending to the long-term economic and mental health effects of policies enacted. For example, in orchestrating the global response, WHO recommendations that turned into restrictions and prohibitions when operationalized triggered paradoxes at multiple levels.

Restrictions and prohibitions to keep the public safe in many cases produced a cost to economies and livelihoods. In developing economies, the paradoxes experienced were even more intense. In these contexts, most work required the physical presence of workers, meaning that social distancing was impractical. Lockdown was also inconceivable for those who had to work today to eat today. Thus, there was a gap between what 'should' and 'could' be done; the former is in principle, the latter is what can be done in practice, which was often far enough from the in-principle position to lay bare the dark side of paradox (Gaim and Cunha, in Pradies et al., 2021). The dark side saw some actors cutting corners and engaging in false mastery. Paradoxes were embraced only discursively but not substantively. Saying was not doing. Organizational conditions restricted some actors' ability to make a legitimate decision when faced with paradoxes (Berti and Simpson, 2021).

Responses to competing demands could also lead to unintended consequences. For example, in their case study of a professional service firm, Padavic et al. (2020) showed that efforts that were supposed to mitigate the work–life imbalance of female professionals (such as flexible work arrangements) usually failed to work. Such efforts could hurt them. When women use policies that provide accommodation in response to distress over work–family conflict, women, unlike men who face the same level of distress, fail to advance. Initiatives to deal with the work–family conflict also reveal the 'thinking-practicing gap' (Gaim et al., 2021) in that 'leaders promulgated a work culture that pitted two fundamental social institutions – work and family – against each other, a culture at odds with the progressive and caring image the organization sought to cultivate' (Padavic et al., 2020: 98).

Padavic et al. (2020) and other authors suggest how diversity, equity and inclusion (DEI) schemes sometimes facilitate structural discrimination that is unintended (see also Mobasseri et al., 2023). Such schemes undermine meritocratic principles (because they are perceived as preferential treatment of women), which ultimately reduces their perceived benefit, especially when such schemes are imposed from the top (Täuber, 2019). True to her prediction that 'blowing the whistle is often denounced' (Täuber, 2019: 1723), a Groningen University academic, was subsequently fired for speaking up[4] (well, for being 'difficult to work with').

---

[4]Christien Boomsma, 'UG can fire social safety expert Susanne Täuber, protest at Broerplein', 8 March 2023. Available at: https://ukrant.nl/protests-against-potential-firing-of-social-safety-expert-susanne-tauber/?lang=en

Another case that focuses on empowering is also illustrative of unintended consequences. The Bright Ideas Campaign,[5] quoting from the programme website, seeks ideas:

> The goal is to get at least one idea from everyone in the organization. For the first idea, each person receives a custom designed coffee cup. The second idea is rewarded with a writing pen. In addition, each week there is a special award ceremony to recognize everyone's ideas. At the end of the celebration management randomly draw names from a basket for one of several prizes. Other award items like baseball caps, gold rimmed coffee mugs, books and medallions can be provided. However, the most coveted prize was a reserved parking space in front of the building.

Well, this may sound quite nice but a little patronising when you read that 'Harley-Davidson ran a similar programme saving $3,000,000 in one 30-day program'.[6] And the distributed ideas' leaders receive a coffee cup! The paradox here is why anyone would bother making their employers wealthier when their employer is disinclined to make the person suggesting 'bright ideas' any better off? What appears to be empowering can disempower in the long term. What is supposed to be participatory can prevent others from participating given the way participation is rewarded.

Box 7.2   Nicola Bulley and the Lancashire police service

On 27 January 2023, Nicola Bulley disappeared while walking her dog in St Michael's on Wyre, Lancashire. Lancashire Constabulary said that there was no evidence of either suspicious activity or third-party involvement in the disappearance. They hypothesized that she had fallen into the River Wyre. However, an extensive search of the river and surrounding land involving police divers, helicopters, sniffer dogs and drones found no body. On 19 February 2023, a couple, walking their dog, discovered a body next to the river, about a mile from where Nicola was last seen. Shortly after Nicola went missing, the police released a statement saying that she suffered from issues relating to alcohol and perimenopause, and that police and health professionals visited the family home on 10 January because of some issues concerned with her welfare. The police issued this statement to explain why they thought it most probable that there was no third-party involvement. The classification increased the priority and resources assigned to the investigation, but the police almost immediately faced enormous social media and mass-media speculation about the case, with the revelation of Bulley's health details being widely criticised by politicians, feminists and the Information Commissioner's Office.

---

[5] Available at: www.chartcourse.com/bright-ideas-employee-suggestion-program/

[6] Available at: www.chartcourse.com/employee-suggestion-box-bright-idea-suggestion-programs-employee-involvement/

What was the paradox in the case of Nicola Bulley? Publicising the details of the missing person's health concerns was a central strategy on the part of the police in trying to diminish wild rumours and speculation as to the likely facts of her disappearance. Many people sought to discover her body, contaminating the crime scene and speculating about who was responsible. Rather than achieving the aim of helping the investigation, the media disclosure had the effect of amplifying social and mass-media commentary, much of it critical of the police for publicising what were seen as private and personal problems, not for general discussion. Rather than helping the investigation, the release of this information made it even more contested as the fog of media commentary obscured the human tragedy (see Box 7.2).

Box 7.3   Good and evil in leaders

Leaders are often perceived paradoxically. In different times and places, people develop different understandings of leaders. For example, Vlad Dracula, the ruler of Walachia, imagined as a cinematic vampire, is portrayed as a national hero in Romania. The real voivod became romanticized as time went by (Moasa et al., 2023).

Genghis Khan, represented as a violent barbarian in many parts of the world he conquered, is depicted in his native Mongolia as the builder of the *Pax Mongolica*, or *Pax Tartarica*, the name used to describe the stabilizing effects of the Mongol conquests of the vast Eurasian territory in the thirteenth and fourteenth centuries. The period describes the eased processes of communication and commerce that the unified Mongol administration helped to create, as well as the relatively peaceful period following the Mongol conquests.

Vladimir Putin, presented at some point as a functional manager of 'Russia Inc.' (Kets De Vries and Shekshnia, 2008) has gained mystical traits. As a stunned oligarch asked minister Sergei Lavrov about how Putin could have planned the invasion of Ukraine in a tiny circle that apparently excluded the foreign minister himself, Lavrov is said to have replied that 'He has three advisers (...) Ivan the Terrible, Peter the Great and Catherine the Great'.[7] He sent his troops to invade Ukraine, first in disguise through his 'little green men' in 2014 and then in February 2022 in full force.

The case of Abiy Ahmed, the Prime Minister of Ethiopia and a Nobel Peace Prize laureate who came to power in 2018, is particularly revealing. When he assumed power in a country that was in turmoil, he was believed to be the bridge between the old and the new. His promises were that he would transcend the aspirations of the newcomers who were assuming power and the fears of the old who were leaving power. Millions were optimistic; he was hailed as the second Mandela, even compared to the prophet Moses. When the nation was politically divided, he preached and practised forgiveness, integration, synergy, reconciliation and bridging opposites. His approach to deal with the paradox of new and old, stability and change was linked to transcendence. In fact, he had written a book, loosely translated as 'synergy', as a manifesto of the

---

[7]Available at: www.ft.com/content/80002564-33e8-48fb-b734-44810afb7a49

government he was leading. With his approach, those who wanted to maintain the status quo were not nervous of the new, while those frustrated with the old were happy to embrace ideas from the past. With majority support unseen in modern Ethiopian politics, he achieved what was thought to be impossible: a peaceful transition of power in the Horn of Africa. He received the Nobel Peace Prize in 2019.

Alas, two years into his government, his mismanagement of the paradox of old and new engulfed Ethiopia in a genocidal war on Tigray, the northernmost regional state in Ethiopia, that has so far killed close to a million people through bullets and starvation. His promise to transcend paradox turned out to be short-lived impression management designed to gain legitimacy and support. The reforms, pardoning of political prisoners, allowing banned opposition parties to join his administration, appointing women to half of the cabinet positions, and making peace with the neighbouring country, Eritrea, all earned him praise and accolades but proved to be a disguise for what he had planned and which ensued: laying siege to the Tigray region of his country. For a Nobel Peace laurate, laying siege to a whole region of 7 million people and sacrificing children and mothers who have nowhere to go, to enrol a few politicians, definitely qualifies him as an evil leader.

The cases in Box 7.3 are all revealing of the complexities and paradoxes of leadership: one's heroes are others' villains and today's angels become tomorrow's demons. Even leadership studies can treat the myths of popular culture as social science (Šliwa et al., 2013; see also Box 7.4).

Box 7.4   Nicolás Maduro, the 'super-bigote'

Many people have a fascination for heroic leaders, and in some cases, some leaders are elevated to the category of myths or even super-heroes. In some cases, this romanticizing is not organic but planned to cause an effect. One of the most interesting cases is that of Venezuelan President Nicolás Maduro. Successor of the charismatic Hugo Chávez, the lack of charisma of Maduro was countered with a number of initiatives, including the creation of a cartoon featuring Superbigote or Supermoustache – i.e., Maduro-as-revolutionary-superhero.

These are available to watch here: https://www.youtube.com/watch?v=XmUyk9krtP o&ab_channel=SuperBigoteManodeHierro.%28Canaloficial%29

https://www.youtube.com/watch?v=bE85dX6XeoE&ab_channel=LuiginoBracciRoad esdeVenezuela

Make your own interpretation of the leadership messages conveyed by the 'super-hero'.

The previous examples are all revelatory of the nuance and complexity of leadership and its temporal effects. Sometimes the impact of measures taken by organizations' representatives become clear only long after the fact. To complicate the picture further, the motives of some leaders are not apparent, especially those person-alities characterized by the traits composing the so-called dark triad (narcissism, Machiavellianism, psychopathy). Under a charming façade they hide unconfessed objectives. Leaders are best dealt with by adopting a paradoxical approach: we should trust them but make the trust conditional by checking them constantly.

Box 7.5   Faster, better and cheaper: the VW emissions scandal

VW's goal in the early 2000s was to become the world's leading car manufacturer with the most satisfied customers and the most satisfied employees. The goal of being the world's leading car manufacturer by 2018 (Strategy 2018) was devised by Ferdinand Piëch, the pioneer of the diesel engine in passenger cars during the 1990s, when VW focused on growth at any price.

In its efforts to conquer the US market, which was crucial for VW to become the world's leading automaker, VW relied primarily on diesel vehicles. Although popular in Europe, diesel vehicles were uncommon in the United States. While diesel engines are more fuel-efficient than petrol engines, for technical reasons they emit greater amounts of nitrogen oxides (NOx) and soot. Complicating the spread of diesel technology in the US market was the 1990 revision of the Clean Air Act, through which the US Congress regulated that all cars sold in the US had to meet much stricter US federal emissions standards.

The challenge for VW was how to balance the internally set growth targets and the increased external pressure, which for the engineers meant developing a diesel engine that was efficient, powerful and clean. In Europe, VW was already leading the introduction of the diesel engine for passenger cars, producing engines with lower noise and odour levels while providing excellent acceleration and fuel economy. However, the fundamental tension between efficiency and performance at the expense of higher emissions remained, even though the diesel engine and exhaust technology were understood to be Piëch's personal ideal of innovation. In an attempt to capture the US market, VW therefore built on the idea of clean diesel, running television ads in the US in 2015 promoting VW diesel vehicles as clean diesel that met US emissions standards. The clean diesel's better performance and lower emissions meant that owners qualified for both subsidies and tax exemptions.

Behind the curtain, the story was different. VW engineers were complaining early on that the California EPA's emissions requirements were unrealistic and nearly impossible for VW to meet, especially when combined with performance and efficiency targets. This proved to be an unsolvable technical conundrum for those who had to deliver the para-doxical promise of a 'fast, cheap and environmentally friendly' diesel vehicle. When VW began developing the environmentally friendly engine, it soon became clear that it could not meet customer expectations and the new, stricter US emissions standards. Rather than admit failure, VW engineers developed software to detect when the car was under-going a test that would then turn on emissions controls. The defeat device made VW's clean diesel appear to balance performance, efficiency and emissions: the TDI miracle. An independent analysis found that the software allowed the cars to achieve lower fuel consumption at the expense of higher nitrogen oxide emissions, with NOx emissions on the road as much as 40 times the standard. This led to the emissions scandal that was exposed on 18 September 2015, when VW admitted that the software had been installed in 11 million cars, 8 million of which had been sold in Europe and nearly half a million in the United States. Although the defeat device – ultimately just a few lines of computer code – cost only a few thousand euros to develop, it led to massive economic damage.

As highlighted in Box 7.5, the VW emissions scandal is a typical example of mismanaged paradoxes where promises and practices misalign. As noted by Gaim et al. (2021: 963) as leaders 'attempt to embrace paradox in the experience of a mission impossible, unwelcome surprises are increasingly likely to occur'. Thus, some paradoxes might not be possible to transcend given their material nature, as was the case in Theranos as well as VW.

How to handle pragmatic paradoxes

When organizational actors are stuck in a pragmatic paradox, their reaction can be reflected in many ways. In the face of competing demands that are difficult or impossible to accommodate, organizational actors may feel emotionally distressed or resort to behavioural withdrawal. A pragmatic paradox might also lead to a sense of absurdity and literal obedience where one knows that doing what is directed won't lead to a desired outcome, but one does it anyway (Cunha et al., 2023a). A case that illustrates this is that of an employee in a less developed country working for a Western multinational which refused permission to allow children to work because of its corporate code. The consequences were to make these children destitute, in a situation worse than being exploited as labour. Of course, neither outcome is desirable, but starving in poverty is even worse than being exploited.

As highlighted above, organizational actors find themselves in a state of pragmatic paradox because of lack of resources or agency (Berti and Simpson, 2021). To help people overcome paralysing pragmatic paradoxes, people need space to discuss impossible orders. They have to think about the contradictions that turn the organization into a paradoxical space. As noted by de Gaulejac (2010), in the face of pragmatic paradoxes, 'reflection is action'. Powerless individuals are supposed to obey even when the order is pragmatically impossible. Of course, this results in absurd processes such as orders that need to be disobeyed to be obeyed, impossible goals that are treated as 'challenging', façades of rationality that cover irrational desires, utopias that come to be condemned as dystopic.

However, organizational conditions might also position actors in pragmatic paradoxes, especially when plurality is not accommodated and linear decision-making expected. Setting stretch goals that would help achieve the personal goals of top leaders can put employees at the bottom in a state of pragmatic paradox (Cunha et al., 2017). Not only will they be emotionally stressed, but the actors will probably resort to cheating to give the impression of accommodating competing demands when non-compliance is not acceptable or penalized (Gaim et al., 2021). In such cases, organizations might find that when they increase their commitment to a losing course of action, they are in an increasingly impossible situation from which they cannot escape (Spicer, 2023).

While generative paradoxes might help organization actors to deal innovatively with tensions and contradictions, pragmatic paradoxes paralyse, leading to problematic emotions, behaviours and decisions (Cunha et al., 2023a). These tensions abound: psychiatrists in the Netherlands (but, we suspect, elsewhere too) have 30-minute appointments with patients and then need 20–25 minutes to complete all the paperwork associated with the meeting (Bal et al., 2023). Because of bureaucracy, experts provide less healthcare quality time. Bureaucracy is one of the main causes of burnout among healthcare providers (Gunderman and Lynch, 2018).

States can also be absurd: in the USSR, there was a 'complex relationship' between official ideology and unofficial ideological rules. The same occurred in Cuba (Cunha and Cunha, 2008). In those contexts, as well as in familiar organizations, 'as anthropologists know well, practices that may appear contradictory to outside observers (or in one context) do not have to be so for insiders (or in another context)' (Yurchak, 2003: 497). Of course, absurdities end up being hyper-normalized, creating a normalization of the absurd (Yurchak, 2003). When illogical practices are treated as perfectly sensible, the absurd becomes normalized, becomes hyper-normal (see Box 7.6). Individuals cope by internalizing the banality of absurdity so that it becomes permanently concealed. Sometimes, a *ritual de lo habitual*, as the Jane's Addiction title goes, is perfectly noticed but represented as the other side of work, which encompasses a purely formal dimension as well as a meaningful part (Yurchak, 2003). A dose of humour or a cynical distance help do the trick.

Box 7.6   The Kafkaesque organization

As noted, organizations often forget about their missions. One factor becomes an obsession. It might be goals, disregarding the role of ethics and values, or it could be rules. When rules become the only thing that counts, the organization risks becoming Kafkaesque. The adjective originated from critical receptions of the works of the writer Franz Kafka. In novels such as *The Trial* (1925) or *The Castle* (1926), he described convoluted, labyrinthine bureaucracies that functioned as 'black boxes' to the general public.

Of course, the prototype is familiar to all: the state machine bureaucracy that sees the public as a mass that moves according to the rules of the machine and not the mission it is supposed to serve. The inner workings of the machine prevail over the (distant) needs of the people.

In extreme cases, the organization develops habits that are shocking to the outside public. In this case, organizations that are created to protect the people become a threat to the people. Security forces become a source of insecurity for the weak (Cunha, et al., 2023b); police forces become violent or corrupt (see Dodd, 2023[8]). The Kafkaesque organization is a reversal of order, a site where the ends become means. It constitutes the epitome of organization as absurdity, a window on paradox.

[8]Dodd, V. 'Met police found to be institutionally racist, misogynistic and homophobic', *The Guardian*, 21 March 2023. Available at: www.theguardian.com/uk-news/2023/mar/21/metropolitan-police-institutionally-racist-misogynistic-homophobic-louise-casey-report

Yurchak (1997) also explored the role of humour and jokes in the normalization of the absurd. The Soviet citizen learned ways to deal with the distance between official and non-official spheres. *Anekdoty* circulated, allowing people to subvert dogmatic truths and to preserve an ironic distance from dogma. The author presents a number of these jokes – for example, the difference between a pessimist and an optimist Soviet is that the pessimist does not believe that things can get any worse, whereas the optimist believes they can. They also managed to know how to take part in ideological practices 'without really being there' (Yurchak, 1997: 184). For example, in large official meetings, people used the meeting to create some free time:

> It was better if the light was dim. Then you could have a nap, or if the light was bright you could read a book. Of course, you tried not to be seen from the presidium because they could reprimand you in front of everyone [...]. But when it was necessary to make some decision, a certain sensor would click in the head – 'Who is voting in favor?' and you raised your hand automatically. (Yurchak, 1997: 172)

People, of course, recognized their contradictory behaviours, but confronting the system looked insane – how can one change the immutable? These resisters were possibly seen as having a 'screw loose' (Yurchak, 1997: 170). Indeed, the Soviet state treated persistent dissent as a psychiatric illness to be cured by imprisonment in the Gulag.

Final note

Despite all the positives that come from embracing paradox, doing so is not easy. In this chapter, we cautioned readers about the allure of paradoxes. As much as managing paradox can lead to great things, mismanaging can mean a disaster. One issue is that managing paradox might be desirable but not possible, due to material limitations. When paradox is desirable but forced, it can lead to pragmatic paradoxes. In the face of the impossible, McCabe (2016) helps us to explain this point in his study of organizations as Wonderlands. The organization-as-Wonderland metaphor means that our expectations of rationality should sometimes be suspended and replaced by the consideration of organization as absurd. When this operation is performed, paradox should be seen not as a source of synergy or renewal, but simply indicating a want of logic. This emerges in several shapes: hoping for A while rewarding B, developing rules that contradict other rules, setting impossible goals to 'motivate people', making claims about social responsibility while expressing social irresponsibility (Gaim et al., 2021), inviting people to speak up while punishing voice (Cunha et al., 2019), defending the importance of employee happiness while creating conditions for their unhappiness (Pfeffer, 2018). Also, now that we have established that paradoxes are produced in power arenas as people communicate, what starts as an absurd situation may simply become normalized as a cultural feature – 'the way we do things here ... '. As Li (2021) explained, we can handle the organizational absurd by reducing expectations and assuming that the organization is simply a strange place.

8

Possibilities and Challenges

The goal in this book is to help create a vision of organizations in which paradox is not a topic for a cabinet of organizational curiosities, but rather an important and integral element in the theory and practice of management. In this last chapter, we will highlight some of the possibilities of integrating paradoxes in everyday organizing and how leaders can nurture an appreciation of paradoxes.

Nurturing an appreciation of paradox

Creating awareness of paradoxes A first challenge for educators and managers consists in creating awareness of paradox. This is important because modern organization theory has been built around the idea of rationality and the removal of uncertainty via systematic, scientific forms of management. Given such a lineage, paradox looks like an uninvited organizational guest, an inconvenient presence. Paradox, in this view, is a symptom of irrationality.

Pioneering work by authors such as Cameron and Quinn (1988) and Lewis (2000) has seen previous forms of 'dysfunction' be reframed as expressions of pluralism and complexity. According to such works, complex, plural systems such as organizations cannot avoid emergence, improvisation and serendipity (Busch, 2022; Cunha et al., 2024; Stacey, 1996). Organizations are thus presented as paradoxical not because they are badly managed, but because complexity is recognized and even appreciated. Thus, visibilizing paradox (as illustrated by the example of Cirque du Soleil in Chapter 5) is a good start in bringing it into the everyday practice of organizations.

Educating organizational members to live with paradox Organizations may educate their members to live with and to embrace paradox – for example, via perspective-taking, which is a tool to integrate different views associated with complex projects. It occurs when 'an individual actively attempts to step outside their own perspective to envision another person's viewpoint, motivation, and emotions' (Edmondson and Hugander, 2023: 1). Perspective-taking forces people to understand the generative potential of seeing through other people's eyes. Doing this creates the possibility that people might make sense of the importance of organizational dimensions that they might otherwise underappreciate. For example, if managers tend to be sceptical about the importance of 'soft' issues, they can be invited to rebalance their views via perspective-taking. Perspective-taking may support collaborations between parties with diverging interests, such as between academics and practitioners (Parola et al., 2022) or, within the same organizational, functional areas with different views or living in different thought worlds.

Promoting balance through governance and organizational practices Organizations are prone to excess, to some extent promoted by senior managers. As noted by columnist Gideon Rachman in the *Financial Times*, we need to distinguish:

> between the actions of, for example, Weimar Germany and Nazi Germany. But the character of a state, and of its leaders, do matter. A Germany run by Hitler or a Russia by Stalin is likely to act differently from when those countries were led by Angela Merkel or Mikhail Gorbachev.[1]

Assuming that individuals will have difficulty in managing balance, especially powerful leaders, it is possible to assume that balance will be better managed by collectives and different powers – namely, governance bodies that impede individual excesses, especially those associated with self-nominated charismatic leaders.

From an organizational perspective, this means creating defence mechanisms against excesses. Governance, through boards, may effectively temper excesses. In democracies, this is operationalized by the separation of powers; in organizations, the same may happen with effective governance systems – namely, executive and non-executive bodies. The role of these governing bodies consists, precisely, in guaranteeing that balance is achieved through understanding paradox not as an individual process but as a collective endeavour. In this view, balance would be achieved not via personal views, but through the balance of powers.

Future challenges

The future of work is being constructed in the present. This ongoing construction is creating a gap with the past. The following themes are illustrative of the difficulties

---

[1]Available at: www.ft.com/content/2d65c763-c36f-4507-8a7d-13517032aa22

facing contemporary managers. These are recent developments in management and organizations that make the consideration of paradox more pressing.

New organizational forms New organizational forms are emerging (e.g., the so-called bossless organization), but old forms persist (Cunha et al., 2022). Most real-world organizations combine elements that are not necessarily well articulated. One government representative described the situation in his sector as combining twenty-first century citizens, twentieth-century technologies and nineteenth-century (bureaucratic) mentality. Organizations are changing as the world changes. New technologies create new organizational arrangements and new ways of working. While organizations are trying to become more agile, agile designs involve some important paradoxical interrogations:

- How can organizations provide autonomy without losing control?
- How can processes become faster without losing reliability?
- How can organizations allow people to make mistakes and learn without damaging their reputation?

New forms of organization are forcing a reconsideration of the meaning of core ideas, such as hierarchy. Some organizations are becoming less hierarchical (Lee and Edmondson, 2017), but reduction in hierarchy is not its elimination. The absence of hierarchy is filled by sensemaking devices. As such, designers need to consider what type of hierarchy or sensemaking device they need and how to make it work. In some cases, organizations can still invest in the traditional forms of command and control while, in others, leadership is invested more in a context designed to stimulate expert professionals to lead themselves. The embrace of new forms of leadership echoes all the questions asked above and confronts designers with the need to find new forms of synthesis between hierarchy and freedom.

Managers in organizations are often confronted by the opposing forces of autonomy and managerial authority (Foss and Klein, 2022). While all managers need to use two leadership gears – namely, the '*exercise authority* mode' and the '*flat* mode' (Greer et al., 2023), the way in which these are combined depends on the organizational context – namely, the type of organizational design in use, the professionalism of the workforce, organizational culture, and so on. Even if the narrative of the bossless company is appealing, it is not realistic for most organizations (Foss and Klein, 2022) that will need to move beyond traditional control mechanisms and find new forms of coordination without obtrusive control. This is, to some extent, an exercise in paradoxical balance. In some cases, it should be noted, new organizational forms, such as agile, are often presented as democratic decentralized, 'cool' cultures. However, at the agile N26 fintech, the top executives accused the cofounders of a 'culture of fear', in which the tendency was to shoot the messenger.[2]

New forms of technologies The emergence of artificial intelligence chatbots such as OpenAI's ChatGPT, Microsoft's Bing, Google's Bard, and X's Grok while they

---

[2]Storbeck, O., 'N26 founders were warned over "culture of fear" at fintech', *Financial Times*, 8 March 2023, p. 6. Available at: www.ft.com/content/167d0b27-ab10-44f0-b82e-52670bbe59a9

can reduce costs and increase productivity, also raise critical issues of ethics and privacy. Such innovations introduce new forms of paradox to organizational life. Technological innovations are creating disruption by clashing new forms of work with established routines. New digital technologies allow the creation of new business models, new ways of working, new consumption patterns. These new developments, such as product-service systems, or servitization solutions, are rife with paradoxical tensions (Bustinza et al., 2019; Hahn and Pinkse, 2022). Servitization, 'the process by which a company expands from selling products and basic services to delivering customized solutions' (Kohtamäki et al., 2020: 1) invites companies to think beyond the product vs service dichotomy. These transformations raise tensions. For example, how can human workers and new automated systems ('robots') work together? How can organizations employ new technologies productively without creating a system of surveillance capitalism? New technologies generate moments of change which raise tensions between established and emerging models.

These tensions are forcing managers to act paradoxically. Some of these paradoxical tensions are nested or intertwined, meaning that as managers strive to solve one problem they may end up producing another. Kokshagina and Schneider (2022) describe the challenge for managers as moving in a 'jungle of paradoxes'. Navigating this jungle is difficult: tensions are intertwined and the effects of addressing one tension over other tensions creates unexpected challenges. How leaders and organizational actors deal with the new digital transformations will thus create conditions to reinvent the way they organize work. Collective action in organizations tends to express characteristics of social dilemmas, conflicts between collective and private interests: actors are supposed to work together to achieve common goals and reach benefits for all, but each member, individually, has incentives not to cooperate. As a result, individuals are often exposed to the tension between deciding whether to cooperate to produce long-term goals or to withhold cooperation to protect personal short-term goals. To complicate matters further, social dilemmas come as 'portfolios', including dilemmas around goals, resources and relationships. In organizational paradox theory language, paradoxes are nested in other paradoxes. This allocation of scarce resources across multiple demands creates a 'controlled chaos' (Rockmann and Northcraft, 2018).

New forms of collaboration and distributed leadership The spread of COVID-19 disrupted ways of life. Organizations had to adapt and accommodate new demands that emerged due to policies imposed to limit the spread of the virus. We have witnessed competitors collaborating, scientists coordinating globally, multi-sectoral collaborations to reach out to the most vulnerable communities, a case in point being the COVID-19 Global Online Hackaton. Similar forms of collaboration have gained traction using platforms (Sarkar et al., 2022). Multi-sectoral platforms illustrate the fact that innovative solutions to existing problems are sometimes available without expert actors being aware of their existence. One case illustrates the point – Patient Innovation, which is a digital platform and online community of users aimed at facilitating the exchange of medical solutions developed by patients. It is a case of a multi-sided platform, in which two or more parties interact directly via a platform.

This platform is a unique case of distributed innovation in healthcare, which is a highly regulated and conservative sector, in which grassroots collaborative innovation is rare.

User innovators develop a new product or service or modify the uses of an existing one. They differ from producer innovators for whom profit is the dominant motive to innovate. Patients and their informal caregivers often developed innovative solutions to help them cope with difficulties associated with their condition, with these solutions frequently improving the quality of life of the patient innovators or their caregivers.

Patient Innovation is a multi-sided digital platform 'created for patients and those who care about them to share and access useful solutions to cope with their diseases'. The case suggests that organizations can encourage innovation opportunities by decentralizing a search. In this view, the role of the centre is to compose and communicate a clear purpose and to create the conditions for the platform to function adequately, a fundamental leadership challenge for our times. In this case, contributing to the well-being of others is a powerful motivation. As a platform for solving people's problems, its non-business approach is positive for the community of users contributing to trying to solve mutual problems. The fact that the platform includes medical scrutiny offers guarantees in terms of the validation of the solutions and creates a communitarian space of non-expert professional users where previously there was none (Oliveira and Cunha, 2021).

Multi-sectoral platforms combine a core mission with ample improvisational space. Open, crowd-based sources of innovation imply a paradoxical combination of *planning* and *serendipity* (Giustiniano et al., 2019). One cannot plan for what is not predictable, and in the case of Patient Innovation, many unpredictable innovations occur. The platform thus constitutes, by design, a space where a *clear end* meets *unspecified means*. Thus, the case suggests that it is possible to create innovation spaces where two types of innovative leadership meet: *the leadership of platform users* and *the leadership of solution providers*. The mission provides the space for improvised solutions to emerge and to gain an institutional context without the political constraints discouraging improvisation in formal hierarchies. Most of these solutions involve recourse to bricolage, making do with the available materials, meaning that the solutions developed by the informal innovators are often frugal (Cunha et al., 2014). Because of the improvisational nature of many projects and their bricolage components, the platform offers the promise of fast action, as improvisation offers a valid path when time to plan is not available, as we saw with the COVID-19 portal. The paradox is that fast action requires access to decision-making powers and resources which patients lack; lacking these powers and resources, innovations require permission from bureaucracy, making the initiative and exercise in futility in terms of its mandate.

New forms of work As we have discussed, the unfolding digital transformation is creating new forms of organization – more distributed, less hierarchical, sometimes described as following a philosophy of 'agile'. These organizations unfold in parallel with new forms of work. These were already unfolding but were accelerated by the COVID-19 pandemic. The pandemic functioned as a 'great reset' (Schwab and Malleret, 2020). Such acceleration forced many organizations to experiment with hybrid forms of work. 'Telework' was not new, but its adoption had languished for decades – possibly because of a combination of tradition, conservatism, resistance to change and fear of losing control.

All these forces that, in Kurt Lewin's language, have 'frozen' the system, have recently been unfrozen by a pandemic that, in a natural experiment, led to a forced change initiative. As these lines were written, 'organizations and employees alike are finding themselves in an uncomfortably liminal state, unmoored from past ways of working but lacking a sense of how best to move forward' (Gratton, 2023: 70). The results of the massive COVID-19 experiment were sufficiently encouraging – or at least not discouraging enough – to convince some managers and employees that the experiment was worth consideration. One authoritative book (Neeley, 2021) that emerged around the pandemic situates the new world of work as follows:

> The rapid and unprecedented changes brought on by COVID-19 have accelerated the transition to remote working, requiring the wholesale migration of nearly entire companies to virtual work in just weeks, leaving managers and employees scrambling to adjust. This massive transition has forced companies to rapidly advance their digital footprint, using cloud storage, cybersecurity, and device tools to accommodate their new remote workforce.

As a result, organizations are now engaging with new forms of (paradoxical) work: presential, remote, hybrid. These alternative forms bring promise, but also some uncertainties (Gratton, 2022) as we enter an unknown future of work. Different organizations are experimenting with different work regimes before they can converge on more stable solutions. What is being learnt from all the experimentation is dynamic. Initially, organizations:

> found that employees often prefer working in a hybrid way and that doing so can build engagement and agility. But now they're also seeing the negative effects that hybrid work can have – on networks and innovation, for example – and they recognize that such problems must be acknowledged and addressed. (Gratton, 2023: 75)

For these reasons, managers will have to navigate a world of uncertainty, one in which practices are diverging: some managers, including Elon Musk, defended the need to go back to work and scrapped the work-from-home policy, stating: 'remote work is no longer allowed, unless you have a specific exception. Managers will send the exception lists to me for review and approval.'[3] Others advocate fully remote working. For example, Neeley (2021) noted that remote work is not a temporary phenomenon but a lasting trend shaping the future of work. Many firms, especially in the tech

---

[3]Available at: www.theguardian.com/technology/2022/nov/10/elon-musk-scraps-twitter-work-home-staff

scene, have made remote work a default option.[4] As the palette of options increases, so does the uncertainty associated with it. The choice of a preferred form will naturally depend on the type of work an organization performs and the technologies in use, as well as on the culture and leadership styles. While each form comes with its challenges, knowledge-based organizations are being pressured to adopt hybrid or remote work. For knowledge organizations, such as GitLab, the future will be one of tech-enabled distributed teams. These teams demand some specific conditions:

- Focusing and measuring output, not input
- Aligning people to norms and values
- Open policies and processes
- Good self-management and people management skills

New forms of work mean new designs, new types of employees, people who are self-starters rather than obedient employees (Sijbrandij, 2023). Management will still be needed but its meaning will change. Being too busy for others will not be perceived as positive, while open-door management will be refashioned (around Teams, Zoom or Slack). In this context, hybrid may be viewed as the best-of-both worlds by some, but by others as the worst-of-both worlds. Regardless of the preferred regimes of choice, in a sense hybridization of work is inviting managers to embrace more *paradox-friendly* modes of leading. Leading implies a combination of presence and non-presence that means that leaders should be 'present' even when they are not present, as well as not being too present even when they are present. Absentee leadership is bad leadership (Hogan et al., 2021) but a 'present' leadership when presence is not welcome can be equally discouraging. Leadership implies a form of contextual intelligence that will be better performed when leaders adjust their behaviour to the specific needs of the situation. This is a form of contingency leadership that now includes juggling online/offline modes and will need to work out how to navigate the transitions between these two modes of work smoothly. The incipient paradoxes of being on-and-off line are evident.

Ideally, leaders will be able to transition between modes with the right mix of being present without being there. Such attention and sensitivity to context may well be a defining characteristic of good leadership. Good leaders are present when they have to be present and leave their people alone when their presence is not necessary (Cunha, 2002). This corresponds to Greer et al.'s (2023) metaphor of leaders as emulating the hippopotamus: most of the time with only their eyes above the water. But even when invisible, the hippo is still there. These leaders, present and not present, attentive to context, will have many new paradoxes to manage. We do not think that the study of paradox and management is likely to be concluded any time soon. The old rationalities are dying where they are not already dead; new, increasingly paradoxical ways of being, working and organizing will continue flourishing.

---

[4]Available at: www.forbes.com/sites/jackkelly/2020/05/24/the-work-from-home-revolution-is-quickly-gaining-momentum/

9

A Final Reflection

As organizations grow more complex, paradoxes will increasingly characterize many aspects of organizational life and individuals' responses to them, forcing people to be 'consciously meandering between the pairs of opposing leadership behaviors' (Gemser et al., 2023: 21). Yet, managing paradoxes is itself paradoxical (Lewis and Smith, 2022). On the one hand, paradoxes offer a way out of polarization and destructive divergence without convergence – the idealistic mission alluded to by Bednarek and Smith (2023). On the other hand, as Xi (2022: 206) observed, 'one may wonder whether humans are doomed when trying to respond to paradoxes', as we seem to be 'chained' to an inescapable web of paradoxical tensions that cannot be solved. As Moschko et al. (2023) observe, dealing with tensional knots is far from trivial.

Examples abound of the non-triviality of managing paradox. Less than two years after attaining B-Corp status, Scotland-based BrewDog's certification was revoked because of revelations of a culture of fear; Emmanuel Faber was forced out as CEO of Danone by activist shareholders unhappy with his focus on sustainability.[1] Managing paradox is a movement in a tight organizational rope. To complicate matters, tensional poles can (and do) evolve, mix and mingle. For example, leaders can become followers and followers can become leaders (Collinson and Fairhurst, 2023). As the arts have taught us, we may see paradox as infinite process, as compositions without beginning or end, for which Guenzi (1996) invites us to think about poet Ezra Pound or composer David Sylvian, as examples. Yet, paradoxical thinking and its associated mindset will help us tackle the most difficult problems (Hameiri et al., 2014). Paradox is a form of managing through dialogue and mutual accommodation, a defining attribute of good organizations and societies (Ragaigne, 2023).

---

[1]Raval, A., 'The struggle for the soul of B Corp', *Financial Times*, 20 February 2023, p. 17. Available at: www.ft.com/content/0b632709-afda-4bdc-a6f3-bb0b02eb5a62

As you will have understood by now, underscored both in theory and the multiple cases and illustrations, the world is full of contradictions and so, not surprisingly, is organizational life. Strong leaders create weak institutions (Rachman, 2022). New artificial intelligence technologies such as Chat GPT promise access to smart information but risk spreading a 'surge of misinformation'. States use illegal organizational vehicles to pursue their unconfessed hidden agendas, Russia's Wagner group being a case in point.[2] The COVID-19 pandemic disturbed supply chains and destroyed organizational plans, forcing organizations to improvise in large scale (Abrantes et al., 2022; Sarkar et al., 2022). Organizations claim the pursuit of social purposes with no adherence to practice (Gulati, 2022) or sometimes in opposition to it, as happened with Theranos, a company whose supposedly noble ideologies (of the 'making the world a better place' type) offered a façade for ignoble ends that demanded people's adherence (Tourish and Willmott, 2023; see Box 7.1 for more details). Non-profit organizations, with their noble missions, are no less immune to scandalous behaviour (Chapman et al., 2023), with some authors hypothesizing that they can be even more permeable to improper actions due to a number of facilitating conditions, including trust, an optimistic view of human nature, fragile governance and moral licensing (e.g., Camps, 2023).

In a polarized political world, companies are in a difficult position. In the US, they are sometimes trying to appease deep-red and deep-blue states: 'Texas telling them they have to do one thing and California telling them they have to do the opposite'.[3] Politics are increasingly contradictory and divisive: companies are pressed to embrace social causes but those seen as too progressive are accused of being part of 'Woke Inc.'[4] Consider climate change. Despite the scientific reality of climate change, strategies of organization sustainability often consist of a form of impression management. ESG goals (environmental, social, governance) are contested political terrain: Wall Street's largest assets managers, private equity forms and brokers regard ESG investing as a threat to financial results.[5]

There are more cases to show that the world, in general, is full of tension and contradiction. These forces, on occasion, are powerful levers of change and renewal, even of beauty. They inform the arts as a space against the ordinary, the known and the predictable. The arts are a preferential context in which to feel paradox emotionally. Arts, such as music, in the best cases offers an emotional, experiential experience of paradox. Nina Simone, performing live in St. Jude, Alabama, in March 1965, in the heat of the events of the Civil Rights movement, expressed 'the conflicting emotions of the marchers themselves: hope and despair, joy and anger, determination

[2]Johnson, M., 'Wagner Inc: A warlord and his lawyers', *Financial Times*, 25 January 2023, p. 17. Available at: www.ft.com/content/8c8b0568-cdd1-4529-a4fd-82e57983ddc5

[3]*The Economist*, 'Command and control', 12 November 2022, p. 63.

[4]*Financial Times*, 'DeSantis' war on woke puts BlackRock on the frontline', 8 December 2023, p. 20.

[5]Temple-West, P. and Masters, B., 'ESG pushback identified as a growing threat to Wall Street', *Financial Times*, 2 March 2023, p. 5. Available at: www.ft.com/content/f5fe15f8-3703-4df9-b203-b5d1dd01e3bc

and weariness'.[6] At other times, paradoxes are absurd and paralysing. Kafka explored this world in his narrative fiction. Paradoxes, as the target of our book, are complex and compelling phenomena that are capable of producing both absurdity and renewal, they are forces that we may try not to see but cannot fail to experience.

How to continue exploring paradox?

Recent years have seen a rich bibliography of paradox, much of which we have discussed in this book. Throughout this volume we have presented many references that will help you find specific materials. In addition to these sources, in case you want to extend your understanding of paradox theory, you may want to consider the following sources. Smith and her colleagues in their edited Oxford handbook offer an exhaustive treatment of paradox in organizations (see Smith et al., 2017b). Smith and Lewis (2022) have recently complemented this academic volume with a book targeting managerial, practitioner-oriented audiences. Berti and his co-authors offered another introduction to organization paradox theory (see Berti et al., 2021), and Gaim and colleagues did the same in a concise volume (see Gaim et al., 2022), both targeting doctoral students and academicians interested in the theme. Advanced explorers may consider Fairhurst and Putnam's book 'Performing Organizational Paradoxes' (Fairhurst and Putnam, 2023). And there are, starting on the next page, the references for this volume.

---

[6]Deusner, S., 'Goddam!', *Uncut*, April 2023, pp. 84–9. Available at: https://pocketmags.com/eu/uncut-magazine/april-2023/articles/1273279/goddam

References

Abdallah, C., Denis, J.L. and Langley, A. (2011) 'Having your cake and eating it too: Discourses of transcendence and their role in organizational change dynamics', *Journal of Organizational Change Management*, 24 (3): 333–48.

Abrantes, A.C.M., Cunha, M.P. and Miner, A.S. (2022) *Elgar Introduction to Organizational Improvisation Theory*. London: Edward Elgar.

Acemoglu, D. and Robinson, J.A. (2019) *The Narrow Corridor: How Nations Struggle for Liberty*. London: Penguin.

Adler, P.S. and Borys, B. (1996) 'Two types of bureaucracy: Enabling and coercive', *Administrative Science Quarterly*, 41 (1): 61–89.

Adler, P.S., Goldoftas, B. and Levine, D. I. (1999) 'Flexibility versus efficiency? A case study of model changeovers in the Toyota Production System', *Organization Science*, 10 (1): 43–68.

Anand, N. and Barsoux, J.-L. (2023) 'Fixing a self-sabotaging team', *Harvard Business Review*, 1.

Andriopoulos, C. and Lewis, M.W. (2009) 'Exploitation-exploration tensions and organizational ambidexterity: Managing paradoxes of innovation', *Organization Science*, 20 (4): 696–717.

Andriopoulos, C. and Lewis, M.W. (2010) 'Managing innovation paradoxes: Ambidexterity lessons from leading product design companies', *Long Range Planning*, 43 (1): 104–22.

Aoki, K. (2020) 'The roles of material artifacts in managing the learning–performance paradox: The Kaizen case', *Academy of Management Journal*, 63 (4): 1266–99.

Ashforth, B.E. and Reingen, P.H. (2014) 'Functions of dysfunction: Managing the dynamics of an organizational duality in a natural food cooperative', *Administrative Science Quarterly*, 59 (3): 474–516.

Bal, M.P., Brookes, A., Hack-Polay, D., Kordowicz, M. and Mendy, J. (2023) 'The absurd workplace: How absurdity is hypernormalized in contemporary society and organizations', *ephemera*.

Bastien, F., Coraiola, D.M. and Foster, W.M. (2023) 'Indigenous peoples and organization studies', *Organization Studies*, 44 (4): 659–75.

Bathurst, R. and Cheng, A. (2023) 'In defense of hesitant leadership: An ancient Chinese perspective', in B. Schedlitzki, M.B. Larson, M. Carroll and O.E. Bligh (eds), *The Sage Handbook of Leadership*. London: Sage, pp. 484–97.

Baxter, J., Hewitt, B. and Haynes, M. (2008) 'Life course transitions and housework: Marriage, parenthood, and time on housework', *Journal of Marriage and Family*, 70 (2): 272.

Bednarek, R. and Smith, W.K. (2023) '"What may be": Inspiration from Mary Parker Follett for paradox theory', *Strategic Organization*, 14761270231151734.

Beech, N., Burns, H., Caestecker, L.D., MacIntosh, R. and MacLean, D. (2004) 'Paradox as invitation to act in problematic change situations', *Human Relations*, 57 (10): 1313–32.

Benson, J.K. (1977) 'Organizations: A dialectical view', *Administrative Science Quarterly*, 22 (1): 1–21.

Berger, J. (1972) *Ways of Seeing*. Harmondsworth: Penguin.

Berti, M. (2021) 'Logic(s) and paradox', in R. Bednarek, M.P. Cunha, J. Schad and W.K. Smith (eds), *Interdisciplinary Dialogues on Organizational Paradox: Investigating Social Structures and Human Expression, Part B* (Vol. 73b). Leeds: Emerald, pp. 27–47.

Berti, M. and Cunha, M.P. (2023) 'Paradox, dialectics or trade-offs? A double loop model of paradox', *Journal of Management Studies*, 60 (4): 861–88.

Berti, M. and Simpson, A. (2021) 'The dark side of organizational paradoxes: The dynamics of disempowerment', *Academy of Management Review*, 46 (2): 252–74.

Berti, M., Simpson, A., Cunha, M.P. and Clegg, S.R. (2021) *Elgar Introduction to Organizational Paradox Theory*. London: Edward Elgar.

Boemelburg, R., Zimmermann, A. and Palmié, M. (2023) 'How paradoxical leaders guide their followers to embrace paradox: Cognitive and behavioral mechanisms of paradox mindset development', *Long Range Planning*, 102319.

Braithwaite, V. (2020). Beyond the bubble that is Robodebt: How governments that lose integrity threaten democracy. *Australian Journal of Social Issues*, 55(3), 242–259.

Burke, C.M. and Morley, M.J. (2016) 'On temporary organizations: A review, synthesis and research agenda', *Human Relations*, 69 (6): 1235–58.

Busch, C. (2022) 'Towards a theory of serendipity: A systematic review and conceptualization', *Journal of Management Studies*. https://doi.org/10.1111/joms.12890

Bustinza, O.F., Gomes, E., Vendrell-Herrero, F. and Baines, T. (2019) Product–service innovation and performance: The role of collaborative partnerships and R&D intensity. *R&D Management*, 49 (1): 33–45.

Cameron, K.S. and Quinn, R.E. (1988) *Organizational Paradox and Transformation*. Pensacola, FL: Ballinger.

Cameron, K.S., Quinn, R.E., DeGraff, J. and Thakor, A.V. (2022) *Competing Values Leadership*. London: Edward Elgar.

Camps, J. (2023) 'Sexual harassment in NPOs: How the nature of work facilitates moral licensing', *Academy of Management Perspectives*. https://doi.org/10.5465/amp.2022.0026

Carlsen, A., Clegg, S. and Gjersvik, R. (2012) *Idea Work. Lessons of the Extraordinary in Everyday Creativity*. Oslo: Cappelen Damm.

Carlsen, A., Clegg, S. and Gjersvik, R. (2012a) 'Generative resistance: How constraints and opposition can inspire your best ideas', in A. Carlsen, S. Clegg and R. Gjersvik (eds), *IDEA WORK*. Oslo: Cappelen Damm, pp. 198–214.

Carlsen, A., Clegg, S. and Gjersvik, R. (2012b) 'Introduction: Why talk about idea work, and what does it matter?', in A. Carlsen, S. Clegg and R. Gjersvik (eds), *Idea Work: Lessons of the Extraordinary in Everyday Creativity*. Oslo: Cappelen Damm, pp. 14–45.

Carmine, S. and De Marchi, V. (2023) 'Reviewing paradox theory in corporate sustainability toward a systems perspective', *Journal of Business Ethics*, 184 (1): 139–58.

Carreyrou, J. (2018). *Bad blood : Secrets and Lies in a Silicon Valley Startup*. New York: Knopf.

Chamorro-Premuzic, T. (2022) *I, Human: AI, Automation, and the Quest to Reclaim What Makes Us Unique*. Cambridge, MA: Harvard Business Review Press.

Chapman, C.M., Hornsey, M.J., Gillespie, N. and Lockey, S. (2023) 'Nonprofit scandals: A systematic review and conceptual framework', *Nonprofit and Voluntary Sector Quarterly*, 52 (1_suppl.): 278S–312S.

Chia, R.C. and Mackay, D. (2023) *Strategy-in-Practices: A Process-Philosophical Perspective on Strategy-Making*. Cambridge: Cambridge University Press.

Child, C. (2020) 'Whence paradox? Framing away the potential challenges of doing well by doing good in social enterprise organizations', *Organization Studies*, 41 (8): 1147–67.

Christie, J. (2020) 'The Post Office Horizon IT scandal and the presumption of the dependability of computer evidence', *Digital Evidence & Electronic Signature Law Review*, 17, 49.

Clegg, S. (1994) 'Weber and Foucault: Social theory for the study of organizations', *Organization*, 1 (1): 149–78.

Clegg, S.R. (2023) *Frameworks of Power* (2nd edn). London: Sage.

Clegg, S.R. and Cunha, M.P. (2018) 'Organizational dialectics', in W.K. Smith et al. (eds), *The Oxford Handbook of Organizational Paradox*. Oxford: Oxford University Press.

Clegg, S., Cunha, J. and Cunha, M.P. (2002) 'Management paradoxes: A relational view', *Human Relations*, 55 (5): 483–503.

Clegg, S., Cunha, M.P., Gaim, M. and Wåhlin, N. (2020) 'The temporal-enduring paradox: The case of Umeå capital of culture 2014', in B. Timo and L. Joseph (eds), *Tensions and Paradoxes in Temporary Organizing: Research in the Sociology of Organizations* (Vol. 67). London: Emerald, pp. 37–60.

Clegg, S., Cunha, M.P., Rego, A. and Berti, M. (2022) 'Speaking truth to power: The academic as jester stimulating management learning', *Management Learning*, 53 (3): 547–65.

Coldevin, G., Carlsen, A., Clegg, S., Pitsis, T.S. and Antonacopoulou, E.P. (2019) 'Organizational creativity as idea work: Intertextual placing and legitimating imaginings in media development and oil exploration', *Human Relations*, 72 (8): 1369–97.

Collinson, D. and Fairhurst, G. (2023) 'Leadership dialectics', in D. Schedlitzki, M. Larson, B. Carroll, M. Bligh and O. Epitropaki (eds), *The Sage Handbook of Leadership* (2nd edn). London: Sage, pp. 484–97.

Cook, E.E. (2019) 'Masculinity studies in Japan', in *The Routledge Companion to Gender and Japanese Culture*. Abingdon: Routledge, pp. 50–9.

Cunha, M.P. (2002) '"The best place to be" managing control and employee loyalty in a knowledge-intensive company', *The Journal of Applied Behavioral Science*, 38 (4): 481–95.

Cunha, M.P. and Berti, M. (2023) 'Serendipity in management and organization studies', in S. Copeland, W. Ross and M. Sand (eds), *Serendipity Science: An Emerging Field and its Methods*. London: Springer Nature, pp. 49–67.

Cunha, M.P., Berti, M., Canhão, H., Barros, P.P. and Fonseca, F.B. (2024) 'Both-and practice in medical practice: Paradox as an adjective not a noun', *British Journal of Healthcare Management* 30 (1): 37–39.

Cunha, M.P., Clegg, S., Berti, M., Rego, A. and Simpson, A.V. (2021) 'Fully embracing the paradoxical condition: Banksy to organization theory', *Organizational Aesthetics*, 10 (2): 50–67.

Cunha, M.P., Clegg, S., Gaim, M. and Giustiniano, L. (2022) *Elgar Introduction to Designing Organizations*. London: Edward Elgar.

Cunha, M.P., Clegg, S.R., Rego, A. and Berti, M. (2021a) *Paradoxes of Power and Leadership*. Abingdon: Routledge.

Cunha, M.P., Clegg, S., Rego, A. and Simpson, A.V. (2024) 'Drawing in the dark triad to teach effective leadership is dangerous, irresponsible, and bad theory', *Academy of Management Learning and Education,* in press.

Cunha, M.P. , and Cunha, R. C. (2008) The role of mediatory myths in sustaining ideology: The case of Cuba after the 'special period'. *Culture and Organization*, 14(3), 207–223.

Cunha, M.P., Cunha, J.V. and Kamoche, K. (1999) 'Organizational improvisation: What, when, how and why', *International Journal of Management Reviews*, 1 (3): 299–341.

Cunha, M.P., Gaim, M. and Clegg, S. (2024) 'Eight paradoxical tensions of organizational improvisation', in M.P. Cunha, A.C.M. Abrantes, A.S. Miner and D. Vera (eds), *The Routledge Companion to Improvisation in Organizations*. Abingdon: Routledge.

Cunha, M.P., Giustiniano, L., Rego, A. and Clegg, S. (2017) 'Mission impossible? The paradoxes of stretch goal setting', *Management Learning*, 48 (2): 40–57.

Cunha, M. P., Giustiniano, L., Rego, A., & Clegg, S. (2019), 'Heaven or Las Vegas': Competing institutional logics and individual experience', *European Management Review, 16*(3), 781–98.

Cunha, M. P. and Putnam, L. L. (2019), 'Paradox theory and the paradox of success', *Strategic Organization, 17*(1), 95–106.

Cunha, M.P., Rego, A., Berti, M. and Simpson, A.V. (2023a) 'Understanding pragmatic paradoxes: When contradictions become paralyzing and what to do about it', *Business Horizons*, 66 (4): 453–62.

Cunha, M.P., Rego, A., Clegg, S. and Giustiniano, L. (2023b) 'In a Kafkaesque catacomb: The killing of Ihor Homenyuk by the Portuguese customs and immigration bureaucracy', *Journal of Political Power*, 16 (1): 23–46.

Cunha, M.P., Rego, A., Giustiniano, L. and Clegg, S. (2023c) 'From a hobby to a business: Drifting through paradox while the business accelerates', *Organizações e Sociedade*.

Cunha, M.P., Rego, A., Oliveira, P., Rosado, P. and Habib, N. (2014) 'Product innovation in resource poor environments: Three research streams', *Journal of Product Innovation Management*, 31 (2): 202–10.

Cunha, M.P., Simpson, A.V., Clegg, S.R. and Rego, A. (2019) 'Speak! Paradoxical effects of a managerial culture of "speaking up"', *British Journal of Management*, 30 (4): 829–46.

Cunha, M.P., Simpson, A.V., Rego, A. and Clegg, S. (2022) 'Non-naïve organizational positivity through a generative paradox pedagogy', *Management Learning*, 53 (1): 15–32.

Cunha, M.P., Vera, D., Abrantes, A.C.M. and Miner, A.S. (2024) *The Routledge Companion to Improvisation in Organizations*. Abingdon: Routledge.

Cunha, M.P., Zoogah, D., Wood, G. and Li, P.P. (2020) 'Guest editorial', *Journal of Knowledge Management*, 24 (1), 1–7.

Davis, J.P., Eisenhardt, K.M. and Bingham, C.B. (2009) 'Optimal structure, market dynamism, and the strategy of simple rules', *Administrative Science Quarterly*, 54 (3): 413–52.

de Gaulejac, V. (2010) 'La NGP: nouvelle gestion paradoxante', *Nouvelles Pratiques Sociales*, 22 (2): 83–98.

de Rond, M. (2012) *There is an I in Team: What Elite Athletes and Coaches Really Know about High Performance*. Boston, MA: Harvard Business Press.

De Vries, M.K. and Shekshnia, S. (2008) 'Vladimir Putin, CEO of Russia Inc: The legacy and the future', *Organizational Dynamics*, 7 (3): 236–53.

Delucchi, M., Dadzie, R.B., Dean, E., and Pham, X. (2021) 'What's that smell? Bullshit jobs in higher education', *Review of Social Economy*, 1–22. doi: 10.1080/00346764.2021.1940255

Denison, D.R., Hooijberg, R. and Quinn, R.E. (1995) 'Paradox and performance: Toward a theory of behavioral complexity in managerial leadership', *Organization Science*, 6 (5): 524–40.

Dobrow, S.R., Weisman, H., Heller, D. and Tosti-Kharas, J. (2023) 'Calling and the good life: A meta-analysis and theoretical extension', *Administrative Science Quarterly*, 68 (2): 508–50.

Dyer, J., Furr, N., Lefrandt, C. and Howell, T. (2023) 'Why innovation depends on intellectual honesty', *MIT Sloan Management Review*.

Edmondson, A. (1999) 'Psychological safety and learning behavior in work teams', *Administrative Science Quarterly*, 44 (2): 350–83.

Edmondson, A.C. (2018) *The Fearless Organization: Creating Psychological Safety in the Workplace for Learning, Innovation, and Growth*. Hoboken, NJ: Wiley.

Edmondson, A.C. and Hugander, P. (2023) 'How to engage skeptics in culture interventions', *MIT Sloan Management Review*, 64 (2): 1–3.

Eikhof, D.R. and Haunschild, A. (2007) 'For art's sake! Artistic and economic logics in creative production', *Journal of Organizational Behavior*, 28 (5): 523–38.

Elberse, A. (2022) 'Number one in Formula One', *Harvard Business Review*, 100 (11–12): 70.

Elliott, J.E. (1980) 'Marx and Schumpeter on capitalism's creative destruction: A comparative restatement', *The Quarterly Journal of Economics*, 95 (1): 4568.

Ettlie, J.E., Bridges, W.P. and O'Keefe, R.D. (1984) 'Organization strategy and structural differences for radical versus incremental innovation', *Management Science*, 30 (6): 682–95.

Fairhurst, G.T. (2022) 'Whither organisational discourse analysis? The case from paradox and leadership research', *Communication Research and Practice*, 1–14.

Fairhurst, G.T. and Putnam, L.L. (2023) *Performing Organizational Paradoxes*. Abingdon: Routledge.

Farjoun, M. (2010) 'Beyond dualism: Stability and change as a duality', *Academy of Management Review*, 35 (2): 202–25.

Farjoun, M. (2019) 'Strategy and dialectics: Rejuvenating a long-standing relationship', *Strategic Organization*, 17 (1): 133–44.

Felin, T. (2014) 'Valve corporation: Strategy tipping points and thresholds', *Journal of Organization Design*, 3 (2): 10–11.

Flyvbjerg, B. and Gardner, D. (2023) *How Big Things Get Done: The Surprising Factors That Determine the Fate of Every Project, from Home Renovations to Space Exploration and Everything in Between*. Basingstoke: Macmillan.

Foss, N.J. and Klein, P.G. (2022) *Why Managers Matter: The Perils of the Bossless Company*. London: Hachette.

Fraser, A., Tan, S., Lagarde, M. and Mays, N. (2018) 'Narratives of promise, narratives of caution: A review of the literature on Social Impact Bonds', *Social Policy & Administration*, 52 (1): 4–28.

Friedman, M. (1970) 'The social responsibility of business is to increase its profits', *The New York Times*, 13 September.

Gaim, M. (2017) 'Paradox as the new normal: Essays on framing, managing and sustaining organizational tensions', (Ph.D. thesis). Umeå University: Umeå, Sweden.

Gaim, M. (2018) 'On the emergence and management of paradoxical tensions: The case of architectural firms', *European Management Journal*, 36 (4): 497–518.

Gaim, M. and Clegg, S. (2021) 'Paradox beyond East/West orthodoxy: The case of Ubuntu', in R. Bednarek, M.P. Cunha, J. Schad and W.K. Smith (eds), *Interdisciplinary Dialogues on Organizational Paradox: Learning from Belief and Science, Part A. Research on the Sociology of Organizations* (Vol. 73a). London: Emerald, pp. 29–50.

Gaim, M., Clegg, S. and Cunha, M.P. (2021) 'Managing impressions rather than emissions: Volkswagen and the false mastery of paradox', *Organization Studies*, 42 (6): 949–70.

Gaim, M., Clegg, S. and Cunha, M.P. (2022a) 'In praise of paradox persistence: Evidence from the Sydney Opera House Project', *Project Management Journal*, 53 (4): 397–415.

Gaim, M., Clegg, S., Cunha, M.P. and Berti, M. (2022b) *Organizational Paradox*. Cambridge: Cambridge University Press.

Gaim, M., Nair, S. and Blomquist, T. (2020) 'Orchestrating ecosystems: Interactive spaces for startup-corporate collaboration', *Management of Innovation and Technology*, 3: 8–9.

Gaim, M., Nair, S. and Blomquist, T. (2022) 'Preparing for your company's first meeting with a startup collaborator', *Harvard Business Review*.

Gaim, M. and Wåhlin, N. (2016) 'In search of a creative space: A conceptual framework of synthesizing paradoxical tensions', *Scandinavian Journal of Management*, 32 (1), 33–44.

Gaim, M., Wåhlin, N., Cunha, M.P. and Clegg, S. (2018) 'Analyzing competing demands in organizations: A systematic comparison', *Journal of Organization Design*, 7 (1): 1–16.

Gaim, M., Wåhlin, N. and Jacobsson, M. (2019) 'The role of space for a paradoxical way of thinking and doing: A study of idea work in architectural firms', *Creativity and Innovation Management*, 28 (2): 265–81.

Gehry, F., Lloyd, M. and Shelden, D. (2020) 'Empowering design: Gehry partners, Gehry technologies and architect-led industry change', *Architectural Design*, 90 (2): 14–23.

Gemser, G., Calabretta, G. and Quint, E. (2023) 'Leadership to elevate design at scale: Balancing conflicting imperatives', *California Management Review*, 00081256231169070.

Giustiniano, L., Griffith, T.L. and Majchrzak, A. (2019) 'Crowd-open and crowd-based collaborations: Facilitating the emergence of organization design', in *Managing Inter-organizational Collaborations: Process Views* (Vol. 64). London: Emerald, pp. 271–92.

Glynn, M.A. (2000) 'When cymbals become symbols: Conflict over organizational identity within a symphony orchestra', *Organization Science*, 11 (3): 285–98.

Gnyawali, D.R. and Park, B.-J. R. (2011) 'Co-opetition between giants: Collaboration with competitors for technological innovation', *Research Policy*, 40 (5): 650–63.

Grabs, J. and Garrett, R.D. (2023) 'Goal-based private sustainability governance and its paradoxes in the Indonesian palm oil sector', *Journal of Business Ethics*, 1–41.

Gratton, L. (2022) *Redesigning Work: How to Transform Your Organization and Make Hybrid Work for Everyone*. Cambridge, MA: MIT Press.

Gratton, L. (2023) 'Redesigning how we work', *Harvard Business Review*, 101 (2): 68–75.

Greer, L., Gino, F. and Sutton, R.I. (2023) 'You need two leadership gears', *Harvard Business Review*, 101 (2): 76–85.

Gregersen, H. (2017) 'Bursting the CEO bubble', *Harvard Business Review*, 95 (2): 76–83.

Grimand, A., Oiry, E. and Ragaigne, A. (2018) 'Paradoxes, modes de régulation et perspectives théoriques', *Revue Française de Gestion*, 274 (5): 71–5.

Grossman, V. (2011) *Life and Fate*. London: Random House.

Gu, Q., Hempel, P.S. and Yu, M. (2020) 'Tough love and creativity: How authoritarian leadership tempered by benevolence or morality influences employee creativity', *British Journal of Management*, 31 (2): 305–24.

Guenzi, C. (1996) 'Music and poetry which evoke nature: David Sylvian and Ezra Pound', *Paideuma*, 25 (1/2): 83–115.

Gulati, R. (2022) *Deep Purpose: The Heart and Soul of High-Performance Companies*. London: Penguin.

Gümüsay, A.A., Smets, M. and Morris, T. (2020) '"God at work": Engaging central and incompatible institutional logics through elastic hybridity', *Academy of Management Journal*, 63 (1): 124–54.

Gunderman, R.B. and Lynch, J.W. (2018) 'How bureaucracy can foster burnout', *Journal of the American College of Radiology*, 15 (12): 1803–5.

Hadjimichael, D. and Tsoukas, H. (2023) 'Phronetic improvisation: A virtue ethics perspective', *Management Learning*, 54 (1): 99–120.

Hahn, T., Figge, F., Pinkse, J. and Preuss, L. (2018) 'A paradox perspective on corporate sustainability: Descriptive, instrumental, and normative aspects', *Journal of Business Ethics*, 2 (148): 235–48.

Hahn, T. and Knight, E. (2021) 'A quantum approach to paradox entails neither preexisting tensions nor asymmetry: Response to Li', *Academy of Management Review*, 46 (2): 362–84.

Hahn, T. and Pinkse, J. (2022) 'A paradox approach to sustainable product-service systems', *Industrial Marketing Management*, 105: 182–9.

Hahn, T., Preuss, L., Pinkse, J. and Figge, F. (2014) 'Cognitive frames in corporate sustainability: Managerial sensemaking with paradoxical and business case frames', *Academy of Management Review*, 39 (4): 463–87.

Hahn, T., Sharma, G. and Glavas, A. (2023) 'Employee-CSR tensions: Drivers of employee (dis)engagement with contested CSR initiatives', *Journal of Management Studies*.

Hameiri, B., Porat, R., Bar-Tal, D., Bieler, A. and Halperin, E. (2014) 'Paradoxical thinking as a new avenue of intervention to promote peace', *Proceedings of the National Academy of Sciences*, 111 (30): 10996–11001.

Harari, Y.N. (2014) *Sapiens: A Brief History of Humankind*. London: Random House.

Harvey, J.-F., Bresman, H., Edmondson, A.C. and Pisano, G.P. (2022) 'A strategic view of team learning in organizations', *Academy of Management Annals*, 16 (2): 476–507.

Hastings, R. and Meyer, E. (2020) *No Rules Rules: Netflix and the Culture of Reinvention*. London: Penguin.

Hay, A. (2022). On the neglect of fallibility in management learning and education: From perfect to adequate managers. *Academy of Management Learning & Education*. amle. 2022.0032

Heller, J. (1985) *Catch-22*. New York: Dell.

Hewlett, S.A. and Luce, C.B. (2006) 'Extreme jobs: The dangerous allure of the 70-hour workweek', *Harvard Business Review*, 84 (12): 49–60.

Hill, L.A. and Davis, G. (2017) 'The board's new innovation imperative', *Harvard Business Review*, November/December, 103–9.

Hillmer, C.K., Roden, S., Vanpoucke, E., Son, B.G. and Lewis, M.W. (2023) 'Radical innovations as supply chain disruptions? A paradox between change and stability', *Journal of Supply Chain Management*. https://doi.org/10.1111/jscm.12299

Hogan, R., Kaiser, R. B., Sherman, R. A. and Harms, P. D. (2021) 'Twenty years on the dark side: Six lessons about bad leadership'. *Consulting Psychology Journal: Practice and Research*, 73(3): 199–213.

Hutchinson, G. O. (2020). *Motion in Classical Literature: Homer, Parmenides, Sophocles, Ovid, Seneca, Tacitus, Art*. Oxford: Oxford University Press.

Independent Directors of the Board of Wells Fargo & Company (2017) *Wells Fargo & Company Sales Practices Investigation Report*. Available at: https://lowellmilkeninstitute. law.ucla.edu/wp-content/uploads/2018/01/WF-Board-Report.pdf

Jacques, R. (1995) *Manufacturing the Employee: Management Knowledge from the 19th to 21st Centuries*. London: Sage.

Janis, I.L. (1983) *Groupthink*. Boston, MA: Houghton Mifflin.

Jarzabkowski, P. and Lê, J. (2017) 'We have to do this and that? You must be joking: Constructing and responding to paradox through humor', *Organization Studies*, 38 (3–4): 433–62.

Jarzabkowski, P., Bednarek, R., Chalkias, K. and Cacciatori, E. (2022) 'Enabling rapid financial response to disasters: Knotting and reknotting multiple paradoxes in interorganizational systems', *Academy of Management Journal*, 65 (5): 1477–506.

Jarzabkowski, P., Lê, J. K. and Van de Ven, A.H. (2013) 'Responding to competing strategic demands: How organizing, belonging, and performing paradoxes coevolve', *Strategic Organization*, 11 (3): 245–80. doi:10.1177/1476127013481016

Jay, J. (2013) 'Navigating paradox as a mechanism of change and innovation in hybrid organizations', *Academy of Management Journal*, 56 (1): 137–59.

Ji, L.-J., Nisbett, R.E. and Su, Y. (2001) 'Culture, change, and prediction', *Psychological Science*, 12 (6): 450–6.

Kahn, W.A. (2004) *Holding Fast: The Struggle to Create Resilient Caregiving Organizations*. Abingdon: Routledge.

Kaplan, S. (2023) 'The promises and perils of corporate purpose', *Strategy Science*.

Keller, J. and Tian, P. (2021) 'The organizational paradox of language', in R. Bednarek, M. P. Cunha, J. Schad and W.K. Smith (eds), *Interdisciplinary Dialogues on Organizational*

Paradox: Investigating Social Structures and Human Expression, Part B (Vol. 73b). London: Emerald, pp. 101–22.

Keller, J., Loewenstein, J. and Yan, J. (2017) 'Culture, conditions and paradoxical frames', *Organization Studies*, 38 (3–4): 539–60.

Keller, J., Wong, S.-S. and Liou, S. (2020) 'How social networks facilitate collective responses to organizational paradoxes', *Human Relations*, 73 (3): 401–28.

Kets de Vries, M.F.R. (2017) *Riding the Leadership Rollercoaster*. New York: Springer.

Kets de Vries, M.F.R. (2023) *The Path to Authentic Leadership: Dancing with the Ouroboros*. New York: Springer.

Kets de Vries, M.F.R. and Shekshnia, S. (2008) 'Vladimir Putin, CEO of Russia Inc.: The legacy and the future', *Organizational Dynamics*, 37 (3): 236–53.

Khan, F.R., Munir, K.A. and Willmott, H. (2007) 'A dark side of institutional entrepreneurship: Soccer balls, child labour and postcolonial impoverishment, *Organization Studies*, 28 (7): 1055–77.

Kleve, H., Roth, S., Köllner, T. and Wetzel, R. (2020) 'The tetralemma of the business family: A systemic approach to business–family dilemmas in research and practice', *Journal of Organizational Change Management*, 33 (2): 433–46.

Knight, E. and Paroutis, S. (2017) 'Becoming salient: The TMT leader's role in shaping the interpretive context of paradoxical tensions', *Organization Studies*, 38 (3–4): 403–32.

Kohtamäki, M., Einola, S. and Rabetino, R. (2020) 'Exploring servitization through the paradox lens: Coping practices in servitization', *International Journal of Production Economics*, 226: 107619.

Kokshagina, O. and Schneider, S. (2023) 'The digital workplace: Navigating in a jungle of paradoxical tensions', *California Management Review*, 65 (2): 129–55.

Kondo, K. & Fukuda, N. (2022) Toyota's business strategy takes a new road with electric vehicles. *The Asahi Shimbun*, April 13, https://www.asahi.com/ajw/articles/14597436, accessed 26.01.24.

Kotter, J. (2012) *Leading Change*. Boston, MA: Harvard Business Review Press.

Krahnke, K., Wanasika, I. and Soltwisch, B.W. (2018) 'The spirit of shinise: Lessons from long-lived Japanese companies', *Global Business and Organizational Excellence*, 38 (1): 6–14.

Kreiner, K. (2020). 'Conflicting notions of a project: The battle between Albert O. Hirschman and Bent Flyvbjerg',. *Project Management Journal*, 51 (4): 400–10.

Lampel, J., Lant, T. and Shamsie, J. (2000) 'Balancing act: Learning from organizing practices in cultural industries', *Organization Science*, 11 (3): 263–9.

Lawrence, P.R. and Lorsch, J.W. (1967) 'Differentiation and integration in complex organizations', *Administrative Science Quarterly*, 12 (1): 1–47.

Lee, M.Y. and Edmondson, A.C. (2017) 'Self-managing organizations: Exploring the limits of less-hierarchical organizing', *Research in Organizational Behavior*, 37, 35–58.

Lei, Z. and Naveh, E. (2019) 'Stuck between two lives: The paradox of eliminating and welcoming errors', *American Journal of Medical Quality*, 34 (1): 92–3.

Lempiälä, T., Tiitinen, S. and Vanharanta, O. (2022) 'Paradox as an interactional resource: An ethnomethodological analysis into the interconnectedness of organizational paradoxes', *Organization Studies*, 01708406221118671. doi: 10.1177/01708406221118671

Lewis, M. (2000) 'Exploring paradox: Toward a more comprehensive guide', *Academy of Management Review*, 25 (4): 760–76.

Lewis, M.W. and Smith, W.K. (2022) 'Reflections on the 2021 AMR Decade Award: Navigating paradox is paradoxical', *Academy of Management Review*, 47 (4): 528–48.

Lewis, M.W. and Smith, W.K. (2023) 'Today's most critical leadership skill: Navigating paradoxes', *Leader to Leader*, 2023 (107): 12–18.

Lewis, M.W., Andriopoulos, C. and Smith, W.K. (2014) 'Paradoxical leadership to enable strategic agility', *California Management Review*, 56 (3): 58–77.

Li, P.P. (2016) 'Global implications of the indigenous epistemological system from the east: How to apply Yin-Yang balancing to paradox management', *Cross Cultural & Strategic Management*, 23 (1): 42–77.

Li, P.P., Liu, H., Li, Y. and Wang, H. (2023) 'Exploration–exploitation duality with both tradeoff and synergy: The curvilinear interaction effects of learning modes on innovation types', *Management and Organization Review*, 1–35.

Li, X. (2021) 'Solving paradox by reducing expectation', *Academy of Management Review*, 46 (2): 406–8.

Liu, H. and Li, K. (2002) 'Strategic implications of emerging Chinese multinationals: The Haier case study', *European Management Journal*, 20 (6): 699–706.

Lovallo, D., Cristofaro, M. and Flyvbjerg, B. (2023) 'Governing large projects: A three-stage process to get it right', *Academy of Management Perspectives*, 37 (2): 138–56.

Luhmann, N. (2018) *Organization and Decision*. Cambridge University Press.

Lüscher, L.S. and Lewis, M.W. (2008) 'Organizational change and managerial sensemaking: Working through paradox', *Academy of Management Journal*, 51 (2): 221–40.

Majchrzak, A., Bogers, M.L., Chesbrough, H. and Holgersson, M. (2023) 'Creating and capturing value from open innovation: Humans, firms, platforms, and ecosystems', *California Management Review*, 65 (2): 5–21.

March, J.G. (1991) 'Exploration and exploitation in organizational learning', *Organization Science*, 26 (3): 327–42.

March, J.G. and Weil, T. (2009) *On Leadership*. Oxford: John Wiley & Sons.

Martin, R. (2007) *The Opposable Mind: How Successful Leaders Win through Integrative Thinking*. Boston, MA: Harvard Business School Press.

McCabe, D. (2016) '"Curiouser and curiouser!": Organizations as Wonderland – a metaphorical alternative to the rational model', *Human Relations*, 69 (4): 945–73.

Milner, J., Milner, T., McCarthy, G. and Veiga, S.M. (2022) 'Leaders as coaches: Towards a code of ethics', *The Journal of Applied Behavioral Science*, 00218863211069408.

Mintzberg, H. (1984) *The Rise and Fall of Strategic Planning: Reconceiving Roles for Planning, Plans, Planners*. New York: Free Press.

Miron-Spektor, E., Erez, M. and Naveh, E. (2011) 'The effect of conformist and attentive-to-detail members on team innovation: Reconciling the innovation paradox. *Academy of Management Journal*, 54 (4): 740–60.

Miron-Spektor, E., Gino, F. and Argote, L. (2011) 'Paradoxical frames and creative sparks: Enhancing individual creativity through conflict and integration', *Organizational Behavior and Human Decision Processes*, 116 (2): 229–40.

Miron-Spektor, E., Ingram, A., Keller, J., Smith, W. and Lewis, M. (2018) Microfoundations of organizational paradox: The problem is how we think about the problem', *Academy of Management Journal*, 61 (1): 26–45.

Moasa, H., Cunha, M.P., Clegg, S. and Sorea, D. (2023) 'Romancing leadership: Temporality and the myths of Vlad Dracula', *Management & Organizational History*, 1–32.

Mobasseri, S., Kahn, W.A. and Ely, R.J. (2023) 'Racial inequality in organizations: A systems psychodynamic perspective', *Academy of Management Review*.

Molecke, G., Hahn, T. and Pinkse, J. (2023) 'Folding organizational paradoxes: Narrative practices for legitimation amid competing stakeholder demands', *Human Relations*, 0(0). Available at: https://doi.org/10.1177/00187267231186532.

Moschko, L., Blazevic, V. and Piller, F.T. (2023) 'Paradoxes of implementing digital manufacturing systems: A longitudinal study of digital innovation projects for disruptive change', *Journal of Product Innovation Management.*

Muethel, M., Frei, C. and Hollensbe, E. (2023) 'Erring professionals as second victims: Grappling with guilt and identity in the aftermath of error', *Academy of Management Journal.*

Munir, K.A. and Phillips, N. (2005) 'The birth of the "Kodak Moment": Institutional entrepreneurship and the adoption of new technologies', *Organization Studies*, 26 (11): 1665–87.

Nair, S. and Gaim, M. (2023) 'How startups can land a second meeting with a corporate partner', *Harvard Business Review.*

Neeley, T. (2021) *Remote Work Revolution: Succeeding from Anywhere.* Boston, MA: Harper Business.

Newark, D. (2018) 'Leadership and the logic of absurdity', *Academy of Management Review*, 43 (2): 198–216.

Nonaka, I. and Takeuchi, H. (2021) 'Strategy as a way of life', *MIT Sloan Management Review*, 63 (1): 56–63.

Oliveira, P. and Cunha, M.P. (2021) 'Centralized decentralization, or distributed leadership as paradox: The case of the Patient Innovation's COVID-19 Portal', *Journal of Change Management*, 21 (2): 203–21.

Ordóñez, L.D., Schweitzer, M.E., Galinsky, A.D. and Bazerman, M.H. (2009) 'Goals gone wild: The systematic side effects of overprescribing goal setting', *Academy of Management Perspectives*, 23 (1): 6–16.

Padavic, I., Ely, R.J. and Reid, E.M. (2020) 'Explaining the persistence of gender inequality: The work–family narrative as a social defense against the 24/7 work culture', *Administrative Science Quarterly*, 65 (1): 61–111.

Palmer, I. and Dunford, R. (2002) 'Managing discursive tension: The co–existence of individualist and collaborative discourses in flight centre', *Journal of Management Studies*, 39 (8): 1045–69.

Pamphile, V. (2022) 'Paradox peers: A relational approach to navigating a business–society paradox', *Academy of Management Journal*, 65 (4): 1274–302.

Parola, G., Spiess-Knafl, W. and Thaler, J. (2022) 'The butterfly effect: How academics and practitioners' micro-practices shape turning points in response to paradox', *Academy of Management Learning & Education*, 21 (3): 369–93.

Patrick, H. (2018) 'Nested tensions and smoothing tactics: An ethnographic examination of ambidexterity in a theatre', *Management Learning*, 49 (5): 559–77.

Peng, K. and Nisbett, R.E. (1999) 'Culture, dialectics, and reasoning about contradiction', *American Psychologist*, 54 (9): 741–54.

Pentland, B.T., Hærem, T. and Hillison, D. (2011) 'The (n)ever-changing world: Stability and change in organizational routines', *Organization Science*, 22 (6): 1369–83.

Petriglieri, G. and Ashford, S.J. (2023) 'Theorizing gets personal: Management academia in the mirror of independent work', *Organization Theory*, 4 (1): 26317877231153188.

Petriglieri, G., Ashford, S.J. and Wrzesniewski, A. (2019) 'Agony and ecstasy in the gig economy: Cultivating holding environments for precarious and personalized work identities', *Administrative Science Quarterly*, 64 (1): 124–70.

Pfeffer, J. (2018) *Dying for a Paycheck: How Modern Management Harms Employee Health and Company Performance – and What We Do about It.* New York: HarperBusiness.

Pierides, D., Clegg, S.R. and Cunha, M.P. (2021) 'Paradoxical ritual and reality in emergency management: An historical approach', *Research in the Sociology of Organizations*, Part 73B: 65–85.

Poindexter, R., Poindexter, R. and Members, J. (1971)*Thin Line Between Love and Hate*. New York: Atco (45 rpm single).

Poole, M.S. and Van de Ven, A.H. (1989) 'Using paradox to build management and organization theories', *Academy of Management Review*, 14 (4): 562–78.

Porter, M. and Kramer, M. (2011) 'Creating shared value', *Harvard Business Review*, 89 (1/2): 62–77.

Pradies, C. (2023) 'With head and heart: How emotions shape paradox navigation in veterinary work'. *Academy of Management Journal*, 66 (2): 521–52.

Pradies, C., Aust, I., Bednarek, R., Brandl, J., Carmine, S., Cheal, J., . . . Keller, J. (2021) 'The lived experience of paradox: How individuals navigate tensions during the pandemic crisis', *Journal of Management Inquiry*, 30 (2): 154–67.

Pradies, C., Berti, M., Cunha, M. P., Rego, A., Tunarosa, A. and Clegg, S. (2023) 'A figure is worth a thousand words: The role of visualization in paradox theorizing', *Organization Studies*, 44 (8): 1231–57.

Pradies, C., Tunarosa, A., Lewis, M.W. and Courtois, J. (2021) 'From vicious to virtuous paradox dynamics: The social-symbolic work of supporting actors', *Organization Studies*, 42 (8): 1241–63.

Prashantham, S. and Eranova, M. (2020) 'Cultural differences in paradoxical tensions in strategy episodes', *Long Range Planning*, 53 (6): 101849.

Putnam, L.L., Fairhurst, G.T. and Banghart, S. (2016) 'Contradictions, dialectics, and paradoxes in organizations: A constitutive approach', *Academy of Management Annals*, 10 (1): 65–171.

Putnam, L.L., Myers, K.K. and Gailliard, B.M. (2014) 'Examining the tensions in workplace flexibility and exploring options for new directions', *Human Relations,* 67 (4): 413–40.

Puyt, R.W., Lie, F.B. and Wilderom, C.P. (2023) 'The origins of SWOT analysis', *Long Range Planning*, 102304.

Quinn, J.B. (1985) 'Innovation and corporate strategy: Managed chaos', *Technology in Society,* 7 (2–3): 263–79.

Rachman, G. (2022) *The Age of the Strongman: How the Cult of the Leader Threatens Democracy around the World*. London: Bodley Head.

Ragaigne, A. (2023) 'Comply while keeping your autonomy, or the art of managing paradox through dialogue', *International Review of Administrative Sciences*, 00208523231158244.

Raisch, S., Birkinshaw, J., Probst, G. and Tushman, M.L. (2009) 'Organizational ambidexterity: Balancing exploitation and exploration for sustained performance', *Organization Science*, 20 (4): 685–95.

Raisch, S., Hargrave, T.J. and Van de Ven, A.H. (2018) 'The learning spiral: A process perspective on paradox', *Journal of Management Studies*, 55 (8): 1507–26.

Raza-Ullah, T., Bengtsson, M. and Kock, S. (2014) 'The coopetition paradox and tension in coopetition at multiple levels', *Industrial Marketing Management*, 43 (2): 189–98.

Riel, J. and Martin, R.L. (2017) *Creating Great Choices: A Leader's Guide to Integrative Thinking*. Boston, MA: Harvard Business Press.

Rigby, D., First, Z. and O'Keeffe, D. (2023) 'How to create a stakeholder strategy', *Harvard Business Review*, 1.

Rockmann, K.W. and Northcraft, G.B. (2018) 'The dilemma portfolio: A strategy to advance the study of social dilemmas in organizations', *Academy of Management Annals*, 12 (2): 494–509.

Rosales, V., Gaim, M., Berti, M. and Cunha, M.P. (2022) 'The rubber band effect: Managing the stability-change paradox in routines', *Scandinavian Journal of Management*, 38 (2): 101194.

Rubin, M., Matthew, F., Miron-Spektor, E. and Keller, J. (2023) 'Unlocking creative tensions with a paradox approach', in R. Reityer Palmon and S. Hunter (eds), *Handbook of Organizational Creativity* (2nd edn). Cambridge, MA: Academic Press.

Sabini, L. and Alderman, N. (2021) 'The paradoxical profession: Project management and the contradictory nature of sustainable project objectives', *Project Management Journal*, 52 (4): 379–93.

Sandberg, S. (2013). *Lean in-women, work and the will to lead*. New York: Random House.

Sarkar, S., Waldman-Brown, A. and Clegg, S.R. (2022). 'A digital ecosystem as an institutional field: Curated peer production as a response to institutional voids revealed by COVID-19, *R&D Management*. https://doi.org/10.1111/radm.12555

Schad, J. (2017) 'Ad fontes: Philosophical foundations of paradox research', in W. Smith, M. Lewis, P. Jarzabkowski and A. Langley (eds), *The Oxford Handbook of Organizational Paradox*. Oxford: Oxford University Press, pp. 27–47.

Schad, J., Lewis, M., Raisch, S. and Smith, W. (2016) 'Paradoxical research in management science: Looking backward to move forward', *Academy of Management Annals*, 10 (1): 5–64.

Schell, S. and Bischof, N. (2022) 'Change the way of working. Ways into self-organization with the use of holacracy: An empirical investigation', *European Management Review*, 19 (1): 123–37.

Schneckenberg, D., Roth, S. and Velamuri, V.K. (2023) 'Deparadoxification and value focus in sharing ventures: Concealing paradoxes in strategic decision-making', *Journal of Business Research*, 162: 113883.

Schultz, M. and Hernes, T. (2013) 'A temporal perspective on organizational identity', *Organization Science*, 24 (1): 1–21.

Schwab, K. and Malleret, T. (2020) *COVID-19: The Great Reset*. Geneva: World Economic Forum.

Seidl, D., Lê, J. and Jarzabkowski, P. (2021) 'The generative potential of Luhmann's theorizing for paradox research: Decision paradox and deparadoxization, in R. Bednarek et al. (eds), *Interdisciplinary Dialogues on Organizational Paradox: Investigating Social Structures and Human Expression*, Part B (Vol. 73). London: Emerald, pp. 49–64.

Sijbrandij, S. (2023) 'GitLab's CEO on building one of the world's largest all-remote companies', *Harvard Business Review*, 101 (2): 30–3.

Silva, T., Cunha, M.P., Clegg, S.R., Neves, P., Rego, A. and Rodrigues, R.A. (2014) 'Smells like team spirit: Opening a paradoxical black box', *Human Relations*, 67 (3): 287–310.

Simpson, A. and Clegg, S. (2024) 'Organizational preparedness, synergy and effective organizational improvisation, in M.P. Cunha, A. Abrantes, S. Miner and D. Vera (eds), *The Routledge Companion to Improvisation in Organizations*. Abingdon: Routledge.

Śliwa, M., Spoelstra, S., Sørensen, B.M. and Land, C. (2013) 'Profaning the sacred in leadership studies: A reading of Murakami's *A Wild Sheep Chase*', *Organization*, 20 (6): 860–80.

Smith, K. and Berg, D. (1987) *Paradoxes of Group Life*. San Francisco, CA: Jossey-Bass.

Smith, W. (2014) 'Dynamic decision making: A model of senior leaders managing strategic paradoxes', *Academy of Management Journal*, 57(6): 1592–23.

Smith, W.K. and Besharov, M.L. (2019) 'Bowing before dual gods: How structured flexibility sustains organizational hybridity', *Administrative Science Quarterly*, 64 (1): 1–44.

Smith, W.K. and Cunha, M.P. (2020) 'A paradoxical approach to hybridity: Integrating dynamic equilibrium and disequilibrium perspectives', *Research in the Sociology of Organizations*, 69 (1): 93–111.

Smith, W.K. and Lewis, M.W. (2022) *Both/and Thinking: Embracing Creative Tensions to Solve Your Toughest Problems*. Boston, MA: Harvard Business School Press.

Smith, W.K., Lewis, M.W., Jarzabkowski, P. and Langley, A. (2017a) 'Introduction: The paradox of paradoxes', in W.K. Smith, M.W. Lewis, P. Jarzabkowski and A. Langley (eds), *The Oxford Handbook of Organizational Paradox*. Oxford: Oxford University Press, pp. 1–24.

Smith, W.K., Lewis, M.W., Jarzabkowski, P. and Langley, A. (2017b) *The Oxford Handbook of Organizational Paradox*. Oxford: Oxford University Press.

Smith, W. and Lewis, M. (2011) 'Towards a theory of paradox: A dynamic equilibrium model of organizing', *Academy of Management Review*, 36 (2): 381–403.

Smith, W.K. and Tushman, M. (2005) 'Managing strategic contradictions: A top management model for managing innovation streams', *Organization Science*, 16 (5): 522–36.

Smith, W.K., Erez, M., Jarvenpaa, S., Lewis, M. W. and Tracey, P. (2017) 'Adding complexity to theories of paradox, tensions, and dualities of innovation and change: Introduction to organization studies special issue on paradox, tensions, and dualities of innovation and change', *Organization Studies*, 38 (3–4): 303–17.

Smith, W., Lewis, M. and Tushman, M. (2016) 'Both/and leadership', *Harvard Business Review*, 94 (5): 62–70.

Snook, S.A. (2011) *Friendly Fire*. Princeton, NJ: Princeton University Press.

Sousa, M., Cunha, M.P., Simpson, A.V., Giustiniano, L., Rego, A. and Clegg, S. (2022) 'Servus or pater? How paradoxical intent can qualify leadership: Inductions from the kingdom of Bhutan', *Journal of Change Management*, 22 (3): 321–53.

Sparr, J.L., Miron-Spektor, E., Lewis, M.W. and Smith, W.K. (2022) 'From a label to a metatheory of paradox: If we change the way we look at things, the things we look at change', *Academy of Management Collections*, 1 (2): 16–34.

Spencer-Rodgers, J., Williams, M.J. and Peng, K. (2010) 'Cultural differences in expectations of change and tolerance for contradiction: A decade of empirical research', *Personality and Social Psychology Review*, 14 (3): 296–312.

Spicer, A. (2023) 'Quagmires', *Organization Studies*, 44 (2): 340–3.

Stacey, R.D. (1996) *Complexity and Creativity in Organizations*. Oakland, CA: Berrett-Koehler.

Sundaramurthy, C. and Lewis, M. (2003) 'Control and collaboration: Paradoxes of governance', *Academy of Management Review*, 28 (3): 397–415.

Takeuchi, H., Osono, E. and Shimizu, N. (2008) 'The contradictions that drive Toyota's success', *Harvard Business Review*, 86 (6): 96–104.

Tan, C. (2023) 'A Daoist understanding of mindful leadership', *Leadership*, 17427150231157450.

Täuber, S. (2019) 'Undoing gender in academia: Personal reflections on equal opportunity schemes', *Journal of Management Studies*, 57 (8): 1718–24.

Ton, Z. (2023) *The Case for Good Jobs*. Boston, MA: Harvard Business Review Press.

Tourish, D. and Willmott, H. (2023) 'Despotic leadership and ideological manipulation at Theranos: Towards a theory of hegemonic totalism in the workplace', *Organization Studies*, 01708406231171801.

Tuckermann, H. (2019) Visibilizing and invisibilizing paradox: A process study of interactions in a hospital executive board. *Organization Studies*, 40 (12): 1851–72.

Uhl-Bien, M., Marion, R. and McKelvey, B. (2007) 'Complexity leadership theory: Shifting leadership from the industrial age to the knowledge era', *The Leadership Quarterly*, 18 (4): 298–318.

Van Dierendonck, D. (2011) 'Servant leadership: A review and synthesis', *Journal of Management*, 37 (4): 1228–61.

Vince, R. (2018) 'The learning organization as paradox: Being for the learning organization also means being against it', *The Learning Organization*, 25 (4): 273–80.

Vince, R. and Broussine, M. (1996) 'Paradox, defense and attachment: Accessing and working with emotions and relations underlying organizational change', *Organization Studies*, 17 (1): 1–21.

Visnjic, I., Jovanovic, M. and Raisch, S. (2022) 'Managing the transition to a dual business model: Tradeoff, paradox, and routinized practices', *Organization Science*, 33 (5): 1964–89.

Vuori, T. (2023) 'Emotions and attentional engagement in the attention-based view of the firm', *Strategic Organization*. doi: 10.1177/14761270231165356

Vuori, T.O. and Huy, Q.N. (2022) 'Regulating top managers' emotions during strategy making: Nokia's socially distributed approach enabling radical change from mobile phones to networks in 2007–2013', *Academy of Management Journal*, 65 (1): 331–61.

Watzlawick, P., Bavelas, J.B. and Jackson, D.D. (1967) *Pragmatics of Human Communication: A Study of Interactional Patterns, Pathologies and Paradoxes*. New York: W.W. Norton & Company.

Weber, M. (1978) *Economy and Society: An Outline of Interpretative Sociology*. Oakland, CA: University of California Press.

Wei, Z. (2009) 'Zhang Ruimin: Awakening the sleeping dragon', in R.J. Pech (ed.), *Entrepreneurial Courage, Audacity and Genius*. London: Pearson.

Weick, K. (1969) *The Social Psychology of Organizing* (2nd edn). New York: McGraw-Hill.

Weick, K. E. (2015) 'The social psychology of organizing'. *M@ n@ gement*, 18(2): 189–193.

Weick, K.E. and Westley, F. (1999) 'Organizational learning: Affirming an oxymoron', in S.R. Clegg, C. Hardy and W. Nord (eds), *Managing Organizations: Current Issues*. Sage, pp. 190–208.

Wenzel, M., Koch, J., Cornelissen, J.P., Rothmann, W. and Senf, N.N. (2019) 'How organizational actors live out paradoxical tensions through power relations: The case of a youth prison', *Organizational Behavior and Human Decision Processes*, 155, 55–67.

Xi, X. (2022) 'Solving paradox by increasing technological capacity: A critique of the concept of business model innovation at TikTok', *Management and Organization Review*, 18 (1): 203–8.

Yurchak, A. (1997) 'The cynical reason of late socialism: Power, pretense, and the anekdot', *Public Culture*, 9 (2): 161–88.

Yurchak, A. (2003) 'Soviet hegemony of form: Everything was forever, until it was no more', *Comparative Studies in Society and History*, 45(3): 480–510.

Zhao, E.Y. and Glynn, M.A. (2022) 'Optimal distinctiveness: On being the same and different', *Organization Theory*, 3(1): 26317877221079340.

Zhou, Q., Dekkers, R. and Chia, R. (2023) 'Are James March's "exploration" and "exploitation" separable? Revisiting the dichotomy in the context of innovation management', *Technological Forecasting & Social Change*.

Zuboff, S. (2022) 'Surveillance capitalism or democracy? The death match of institutional orders and the politics of knowledge in our information civilization', *Organization Theory*, 3 (3): 26317877221129290.

Index

Page numbers in **bold** refer to boxes, those in *italics* indicate figures.

Ubuntu 45–7
undecidability 13, 54
unintended consequences of (mis)management
    75–81
US and Swedish culture, compared 48–9

Valve: rule of three 33
vicious and virtuous circles 58, 60, 61
visualizing competing demands 16–18
voluntary vs forced choices 58–60
VW emissions scandal 73, **80–1**

weak vs strong paradoxes 61–2
Weick, K. 18, 22
Western and Eastern philosophical traditions
    43–5
work, new forms of 88–90
work–family conflict 76
work–life balance 48–9, 62, **63–4**, 69

yin–yang symbol 17–18, 44–5
Yurchak, A. 82–3